Praise for *Powerful C*

"Whether you are just starting your evidence-informed journey or already well on the way, *Powerful Classrooms* is filled with strategies and insights that will help you on your path to a truly powerful classroom. Bain's unique perspective is buoyed by a multitude of diverse educators' voices and evidence-informed approaches, making this book an invaluable resource."

—*Kent Wetzel, leadership development teacher specialist, Frederick County Public Schools, Maryland*

"As an education practitioner determined to improve learner outcomes, you'll definitely sense the golden thread running throughout this book; that every teacher can be successful if they appreciate the impact that comes from teaching students how to learn. Patrice Bain has unselfishly made life so much easier for all of us, by providing further "evidence" for the science of learning, both through her own significant classroom research, and by capturing the voices of other educational influencers who use evidence-based strategies to create intentional classrooms."

—*Liz Keable, "Metacognition in Practice" specialist*

"This book delivers what teachers really need to transform research into reality – concrete examples from Patrice's own pioneering experience combined with other teachers' insights from their own powerful classrooms."

—*Diane Lauer, chief academic officer, St. Vrain Valley Schools, Colorado*

"In a perfect world, every teacher would have an evidence-informed expert and friend in the classroom next door to generously share the most powerful teaching strategies! Patrice Bain is that best friend and teaching colleague. In *Powerful Classrooms*, she not only delivers the best, most actionable evidence-informed advice and guidance, but she also introduces the reader to her friends – creating an inspiring community of expertise within a book that will become a trusted companion."

—Margaret (Meg) Lee, educator, connector, and author of
Mindsets for Parents

"Patrice Bain is a teacher's teacher. By telling her own journey in cognitive science, her book is a celebration of teachers across the world who have embraced the science of learning in their classrooms. This is a must-read, how-to manual for any educator looking to better inform their practice with what scientists know about how we learn."

—M-J Mercanti-Anthony, Ed.D, principal, Antonia Pantoja
Preparatory Academy, NYC Public Schools

"Patrice has done it again! *Powerful Classrooms* is an essential guide that bridges cognitive science and classroom practice, offering educators evidence-based strategies that we can start using straight away. Teachers who caught the bug with the first *Powerful Teaching* book will find this companion filled with tools, tips, and resources, all enriched by Patrice"s deep experience as a master teacher. Where was this book when I was in teacher school?"

—Zach Groshell, PhD, teacher, instructional coach, host of the
Progressively Incorrect podcast

"*Powerful Teaching* inspired you to embrace the messiness of learning. *Powerful Classrooms* by Patrice Bain builds on this foundation by equipping you with concrete, innovative strategies that help you navigate this complexity. These strategies not only acknowledge the intricacies of modern education but actively harness them to enhance student engagement and learning outcomes. This book is your essential guide to transforming classroom challenges into opportunities by mastering the beautiful chaos of real learning."

—Shannon Schinkel, high school educator and host,
The Embrace the Messy Podcast with Shannon Schinkel

Powerful Classrooms

Powerful Classrooms

Evidence-informed Strategies and Resources

Patrice M. Bain, Ed.S.

JB JOSSEY-BASS™
A Wiley Brand

To Mark and Roddy
For pursuing the idea of conducting research in classrooms

To Pooja
Who helped turn research into reality

To Amber
*And all teachers who embrace and bring the science
of learning to their students*

To Suzy and Shane
For the spark that inspired me to write this book

To Steven
My forever

Contents

Contents

Foreword

In my work I have the privilege of meeting hundreds of teachers in different school contexts. I also have the honor of watching them in action, wrestling with the everyday challenges of running classrooms so that their students are all thriving – socially and emotionally and also in terms of their learning. As I sit at the back of the room, I'm often struck by the thought that teaching is a truly extraordinary process: setting out a set of ideas and activities that allow each and every child across a class to make sense of new concepts and skills and to build confidence using them. It's a universal feature of great teachers that they foster relationships infused with kindness and respect: they seek to inspire and motivate. Teachers are generally wonderful people seeking to do good! But even if it looks artful and effortless on the surface, it's not ever easy. In practice, teaching groups of children successfully all at once is a very significant challenge for everyone.

This isn't so much because each child is so different in the way they learn – as Dan Willingham says, we are more alike than different in this regard. The challenge arises because of the inherent common difficulties all learners experience – that our working memories are limited, we can only handle a small amount of information at a time, and we are prone to forgetting a lot of what we first encounter. Added to this, our students arrive with such varying levels of prior knowledge and emotional responses to success and failure, and it's logistically complicated to check in on how multiple people are doing, all at one time, finding out how they have made sense of the material we're trying to teach.

Fortunately, help is at hand! Learning processes have been extensively researched and, increasingly, teachers are exploring how to implement ideas from research in their day-to-day practice. Patrice Bain has been at the forefront of this work for many years. I've enjoyed hearing her tell the story of researchers coming to study her classroom a few times and it's never short of totally inspiring! Her book *Powerful Teaching*, written with Pooja Agarwal, represents a perfect example of research and practice developing in tandem, each influencing the other. This is exactly the kind of information and inspiration that teachers need.

As a full-time teacher trainer and author of the series *Teaching WalkThrus*, where my colleague Oliver Caviglioli and I have tried to communicate a wide range of well-known teaching ideas via some five-step visual guides, I know from firsthand experience just how hard it is for teachers to take ideas from a book, written by someone else, and translate them into practice in their own contexts – their classroom, their children, their subject, their school. What people often cry out for are examples. The concepts can be interesting in theory – they are intellectually rewarding to discuss and explore. But the vital question is: What does this look like in practice?

In this epic book, Patrice has pulled so many ideas together with example after example – it's quite remarkable. I'm absolutely certain that teachers of children at every age, in schools all around the world, will find the ideas and suggestions here incredibly valuable. If teachers are anything like me, even a surface browse will be making their brains fizz with ideas. But as they stop to read more slowly, they'll find that Patrice has laid out a clear path for them, linking the fundamental ideas from research to the nuts and bolts of specific lesson sequences. This means that, when trying to implement the ideas, teachers are always clear on the reasoning behind them. In my work, I find this is vital. It's much more likely that techniques will become embedded as solid, effective routines if teachers are clear about their purpose from the start.

A final point to note about this fabulous book is the rather brilliant and highly original final section about influencers and sources of inspiration. Each contributor has set who influences them in the world of cognitive science, coupled to some references to their own work. Patrice is giving people space to honor the work of others in a manner that is absolutely typical of her generosity of spirit and her determination to spread the love for educational research and evidence-informed teaching.

It's been a significant honor to meet and talk to Patrice about her work and I'm delighted to have been asked to make a contribution to this book; I know for sure it will find a wide audience. This means that a lot of children are going to end up learning more and enjoying school more, finding inspiration in their personal learning journeys – and there's nothing more exciting or important than that!

Tom Sherrington, author and Director of Teaching
WalkThrus International

Introduction

Welcome to *Powerful Classrooms: Evidence-informed Strategies and Resources*.

"I wanted to shout from the mountaintops that the science of learning works." Writing in *Scientific American*, Annie Murphy Paul used these words of mine as one of the big takeaways from our interview. *Powerful Teaching: Unleash the Science of Learning*, by Dr. Pooja Agarwal and me, was released in 2019, and since then I've been on the hike up that mountain, speaking on podcasts and presenting at many conferences and professional development sessions for educators, in person and virtually, across the globe. I have intentionally used social media to spread what

I know and what other teachers using scientifically proven strategies have learned. I hope you will join us on this hike and help get us to a promontory where each teacher can shout this new knowledge down to your chosen valley.

This book is a resource. It is a companion to *Powerful Teaching*, but written in my teaching voice. I wanted to create a place where teachers had access to a multitude of strategies at their fingertips. I describe research and why it works and I discuss it through my own eyes, my words, and what I experienced working alongside cognitive scientists in my classroom. I highlight teachers, leaders, and instructional coaches from around the world who have incorporated evidence-informed teaching into pedagogy. I feature my edu-heroes, my influencers – many of those I have followed for years.

Learning is messy and I invite you to be messy with this book. Like something? Dog-ear the page. Write in the margins. I practice what I preach and hope you will complete the exercises that go along with each chapter. Keep your pencil handy. Adapt the strategies to fit your students. The final chapter is a Do-It-Yourself Retrieval Guide. Feel free, at the end of each chapter, to use the strategy of retrieval to complete a section in this Guide. Or perhaps you might like to try spaced retrieval and, by waiting until you have finished the book, quiz yourself to see how much you are able to retrieve. You may also want to use it in a Book Study. It's your book.

And most of all, thank you for joining me in this grand adventure of learning. I hope you will ponder my ideas and experiences, and accompany me and my like-minded heroes who are changing the way research, learning, and teaching are making their way to the mountaintops.

Chapter 1

How It Started

How often have we had the opportunity to be in the room, at the table, when a revolution begins? And, how often in our naivete do we simply navigate the waters, doing what needs to be done, and not realizing the enormity of what happened in that room until years later? Emerging before our eyes is a learning revolution based on cognitive science and robust research. The research began in my own classroom, and what scientists learned there is making its way around the globe.

HERE'S MY BACK STORY

My teaching career began in a small school district in southern Illinois, USA, in the early 1990s. My subject was World History, appearing in our curriculum for sixth graders for the first time. I had an incredible principal, Dr. Roger Chamberlain, who believed in encouraging his faculty to soar. I was also very fortunate to have a forward-thinking and fair superintendent, Mr. Jack Turner, and a like-minded school board. Because of their encouragement, I sought opportunities, and was rewarded by being named a Finalist for Illinois Teacher of the Year in 2000, and a European Fulbright Scholar in 2004. However, after having taught for over 12 years, enjoying opportunities stemming from teaching awards, and finishing an advanced educational degree, I was perplexed. The majority of my students received excellent grades, yet some did not. Why?

I didn't know the "how" nor the "where" of learning to answer the "why" for the differences in success between my students. Up until this time, most research on learning in the United States had been conducted at universities, in laboratories, with college students. The scholarly papers were published in academic journals and the findings were locked in ivory towers. And even though, at this time, I also served as adjunct faculty at two local universities teaching pedagogy to instructors pursuing advanced degrees, I wasn't aware this information existed. An epiphany arose: I had been taught how to teach, and I taught others how to teach, but I had no idea how we learn.

I had a serendipitous meeting with Dr. Mark McDaniel, a cognitive scientist at Washington University in St. Louis, Missouri. He was researching memory and, for the first time, I began to see a connection between learning and the science of memory formation. Could this be the link to success for the students who were not doing well? Dr. McDaniel introduced me to Dr. Henry Roediger, another cognitive scientist from Washington University. (McDaniel and Roediger are authors of a wonderful book about learning: *Make It Stick*.) I was not aware of their credentials nor expertise; in fact, even the term "cognitive scientist" was lost on me. To me, they were simply Mark and Roddy. (In hindsight, I shake my head at the audacity!) I remember having them over to my house in the country, enjoying a glass of wine on the porch amidst the trees, as conversations continued. I told them of my frustrations at the disconnect between teaching and learning. They discussed their research ideas. The lightbulb moment happened: they wanted to study how students learn in an authentic, public-school classroom. Would I consider a research study in my classroom? My immediate thought was that this might not only be the answers to my questions but could also benefit my underperforming students.

Many stakeholders were involved in deciding whether the study would go forward. Satisfying my district's administration, getting the community's support, and funding became steps along the path. Meetings with my school administration ensued. A question from my superintendent became my focus: *Why* do you want this? I answered with conviction, "I want to know how my students learn." Roediger and McDaniel obtained funding through the Institute of Education Sciences and my administration gave its approval. I obtained permission from the parents of my students, and in August 2006, we were ready to begin.

On that August day I met another researcher from Washington University, Pooja Agarwal. As we climbed the staircase to my classroom, we pondered. Where should we begin? We knew the focus of the study would be testing (which we now refer to as retrieval). There were no classroom studies for us to replicate. Many new conditions needed to be taken into account, which were nonexistent in university laboratory settings, such as fire drills, tornado drills, student absences, and the frequent interruptions of the overhead speaker: "Mrs. Bain, will you please send (student's name) to the office; he is leaving for an appointment." And, of course, because we were working with adolescents, we needed to consider how drama, divorcing parents, ill grandparents, etc., had an impact on learning. Designing research for a classroom required looking at a multitude of variables.

Since Pooja and I were in the best position to see the whole picture, we were granted the autonomy to create our ideas and take them to the Washington University cognitive scientists for their input and approval. For the first semester, 18 weeks, Agarwal was in my class daily, observing my teaching. We had weekly meetings to devise research methods. To me, this process was invaluable. I was not expected to change my teaching to fit the research design; rather, the design was of mutual respect for the research, the teaching, and the students. In January 2007, the research on retrieval (as measured and encouraged by testing) began.

Later that year, I was invited to be the sole US K–12 teacher to work with cognitive scientists, in conjunction with the Institute of Education Sciences in Washington D.C., writing *Organizing Instruction and Study to Improve Student Learning.*[1] Once again, I had the good fortune to have a seat at the table. The recommendations emerging from this guide gave me clues for designing further experimental research with my students. For the next few years, Dr. Agarwal and I studied how spaced practice, interleaving, and feedback-driven metacognition played a role in retrieval and learning. I saw firsthand how my students flourished using the methods we studied. And I saw how they went from a simple recall of facts to deep and critical thinking; this allowed me to devise and develop strategies based upon the research.

About ten years after the research started in my classroom, I had a clear vision of exactly what our research had accomplished. Through robust research we had shown that grades, learning, and knowledge retention showed great gains using our results. I had another epiphany. It wasn't *me*, the teacher, making this difference. It was the research and evidence-informed methods and strategies I was using. I wanted to shout from a mountaintop: *every* teacher, no matter where in the world the classroom might be, could have the same success with students. People began to take notice of the research. Annie Murphy Paul spent a day in my class, observing my teaching and talking with my students for an article in *Scientific American*. A camera crew filmed a day in my class for a PBS (Public Broadcasting

System) NOVA documentary: "The School of the Future." For several years I worked with REL (Regional Educational Lab) Mid-Atlantic giving presentations to teachers in Pennsylvania, Maryland, Delaware, and New Jersey. My co-presenters included Dr. Hal Pashler, Dr. Ken Koedinger, and Dr. Nate Kornell. I was interviewed along with Dr. Henry Roediger and one of my students, Zoe Hejna, for an NPR (National Public Radio) program. And finally, to document our story, and provide a map for others to follow, Dr. Agarwal and I published *Powerful Teaching: Unleash the Science of Learning*.[2] The purpose of my next publication: *A Parent's Guide to Powerful Teaching*[3] was to assist teachers in having a learning dialogue with parents and caregivers, in addition to helping families understand how learning happens and providing strategies for helping with schoolwork at home.

The learning revolution and research continue. What began in my classroom has expanded into many schools. A meta-analysis and research database can be found at Retrieval Practice.[4] My bookshelves are filled with books rooted in cognitive science and the authors feel like kindred spirits. What was once tucked away in journals and ivory towers is now available to all. Each time a teacher reads a research and evidence-based book, attends professional development on the science of learning, listens to a related podcast, and incorporates the findings in the classroom, another seat is added to the table and the number of participants in this revolution increases.

And as we encounter new teaching methodologies, our new standard and duty is to ask, "On what evidence is this based?"

Little did I know that my simple question, "How do we learn?" would be answered by science-based methods that have spread globally, and have become mainstream for many. My curiosity about learning led to answers that enabled me to begin the first day of every school year with: "I'm your teacher and I'm going to teach you how to learn," because I *know* it works. I was in the room where it happened.

NOTES

1. Pashler, Harold, Patrice M. Bain, Brian A. Bottge, Arthur Graesser, Kenneth Koedinger, Mark McDaniel, and Janet Metcalf. *Organizing Instruction and Study to Improve Student Learning.* Washington, D.C.: National Center for Educational Research, Institute of Education Sciences U.S. Department of Education, 2007.

2. Agarwal, Pooja K., and Patrice M. Bain. *Powerful Teaching: Unleash the Science of Learning.* San Francisco: Jossey-Bass, 2019.

3. Bain, Patrice M. *A Parent's Guide to Powerful Teaching.* Woodbridge: John Catt Publishing, 2020.

4. Retrieval Practice. Database of retrieval practice research. Available at: https://www.retrievalpractice.org/strategies/2019/10/28/database-of-retrieval-practice-research [Accessed 10 May 2024].

Chapter 2

The Research

RESEARCH IN MY CLASSROOM

Let me begin with a confession. I don't enjoy reading research papers. As a very busy teacher, I maintained the "one-minute rule": If my interest wasn't piqued in one minute, I moved on. (Which is why I am very grateful to researchers, like Dr. Pooja Agarwal, Dr. Erika Galea, Dr. Nidhi Sachdeva . . . and many more, who sift through studies and give us what's important in bite-sized chunks.)

Yet we all know research is vital to our profession and aids student learning. I saw lightbulbs of learning click on in my students' eyes as I applied the conclusions of scientific studies in my class. Since 2007, many articles and papers (and even a book: *Powerful Teaching!*) discuss the very research that happened in my classroom.[1] What follows, however, are my words, describing the research in layperson's terms, discussing the research from a teacher's point of view. You may wish to replicate the study in your own classroom, or simply apply the methods and watch the results.

Here is a glimpse into my classroom. My school was located in a small district in southern Illinois. At the middle-school level where I taught, students had different teachers for different subjects, each one specializing in math, science, language arts, social studies, art, music, or physical education. I taught social studies to 6th graders (~11-year-olds), with the focus on World History. In my school district's curriculum, this was the students' introduction to the subject; the majority of my students did not possess background knowledge. Students used textbooks that consisted of overall units (e.g. ancient river civilizations), broken down into chapters (e.g. Nile, Tigris/Euphrates, Indus, and Huang). The chapters were broken down into lessons (e.g. geography, history, ways of life, etc.). My methods of teaching included reading, lecture, presentations, storytelling, and projects. I had six classes each day with an average of about 22 students per class.

At the start of the research, we (researcher Pooja Agarwal and I) spent a semester looking at retrieval, or the bringing forth of information students had previously learned. Our hypothesis was that retrieval was effective; but how could we design a study around it? A clear choice could have been exposing some of the students to retrieval and others not. Yet, if the hypothesis was that retrieval enhances learning, that option did not feel ethical. Why would we offer benefits to some students while denying those benefits to others? This called for a change in action; rather than *who* was a control group, our answer became *what* was the control group.

The control group became the questions on my chapter tests for which students had not practiced retrieval. The experimental group became the questions on the test on which retrieval was to be used.

Here is how we introduced the strategy of retrieving material into the class. Prior to beginning a unit, I gave a copy of the chapter exams to Ms. Agarwal (who later became Dr. Agarwal). She divided the exam questions into two sets:

1. Control group (no retrieval).
2. Experimental group (those items which would be retrieved, via quizzes, prior to the exam).

The method for quizzing was the use of multiple-choice questions via clickers. Each of my six daily classes received a different set of retrieval questions on these quizzes. There were two to three clicker quizzes given throughout the course of the chapter being studied, thus also incorporating spacing. (More information on retrieval and spacing is found in Chapter 4.) To ensure I could not influence the outcome, I was never privy to which exam questions would be retrieved in the quizzes and which questions would not be retrieved. Moreover, I was never in the classroom when the retrieval quizzes were given; Ms. Agarwal handled the quizzes and data.

I taught all of my classes and gave the chapter tests, as usual. After I had graded the tests and gone over them with the students, Ms. Agarwal took the students' papers and compiled the data.

Here are some of the results:

Experiment 1

<u>% of Correct Answers on Retrieved vs. Nonretrieved Exam Questions</u>

Chapter	Retrieved Questions (%)	Nonretrieved Questions (%)
4	93.0	83.0
5	93.0	79.0
6	91.0	81.0
7	84.0	82.0
Mean of 4, 5, 6, 7	90.25	81.25

(continued)

(*continued*)

According to the experiment design for chapters 4–7, questions for the multiple-choice chapter exams were divided into two groups: retrieved questions (experimental group 1) and nonretrieved questions (control group). A total of **492 chapter exams** were used for the data for this portion of Experiment 1.

As we pondered the research, a thought occurred. Are the students scoring higher simply because they had seen the material of the tested questions an additional time? This led to another experiment – Experiment 2. Our hypothesis was: If "seeing" the information was as effective as retrieval, scores should be the same. During these clicker quizzes, some of the questions required retrieval, but others simply presented material again, without retrieval being required. Students saw a correct fact on the board; however, there were no multiple-choice items for them to choose. For example, see a screenshot of what a "read-only" statement looked like.

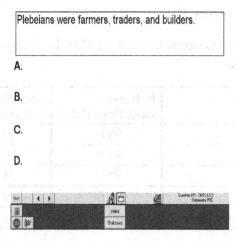

Experiment 2

Percentage of correct chapter exam answers on retrieved (quizzed), read-only (but not retrieved), and nonretrieved (never quizzed) exam questions.

Chapter	Retrieved Questions (%)	Read-only Statements (%)	Nonretrieved Questions (%)
9	91.0	83.0	81.0
13	59.0	53.0	54.0
Mean of 9, 13	75.0	68.0	67.5

The second table compares the mean of correct answers for the experimental group 1 (retrieved questions), experimental group 2 (read-only Statements), and the control group (nonretrieved questions) for each chapter. The second table also shows the mean of correct answers of experimental group 1, experimental group 2, and the control group for all **245 exams**.

The conclusion I reached: Visually exposing students once more to concepts during the course of study offers a higher score over no additional exposure. However, giving students the opportunity to retrieve material prior to exams leads to higher retention of material.

Time to Ponder. . .

If "retrieving" information is more effective than simply "seeing" the information, how can you create learning environments that incorporate retrieval and spacing?

As the end of the first semester of our retrieval research was winding down, we had clearly seen the benefit of using retrieval throughout the course of study. In the graph, the "End of the Chapter" was quite typical of what we had seen, chapter after chapter. However, one day we asked ourselves, "We know retrieval works at the end of chapters; how much will students remember at the *end of the year*? And, what if we gave them an unannounced test that covered material from all semester?" The idea of a "pop final" was born, meaning the students had no advanced knowledge and therefore did not study. This was an opportunity to test for retrieval over several months' worth of material. For fairness, the scores did not go into my gradebook. See the "End of the Semester" results in the graph.

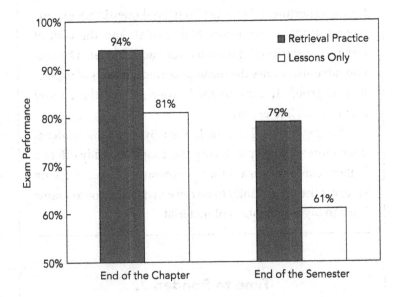

Again, I wanted to shout from the mountaintop. Without any time spent on class review or at-home study, my students retained, on average, 79% of what I had taught.

The research results motivated me. I had clear proof that retrieval and spacing increased learning and knowledge retention. What strategies could I create that would tie in with the research? This is the time I developed the ideas for the Four Steps of Metacognition, Retrieval Cards, Retrieval Guides, and Mini-quizzes (see Chapter 6 on Strategies). What was becoming clear was that ALL of my students were thriving, regardless of their ability level. In fact, it was the struggling students and students in special education classes who made the greatest gains. My mantra became: I'm your teacher and I'm going to teach you *how to learn*.

After Ms. Agarwal was no longer recording data with my classes, I wanted to conduct my own research. I began each lesson with a pre-test. (There were usually four to five lessons per chapter.) Because the majority of my students had little or no prior knowledge, I used pre-tests as a way to provide a base and the questions provided me an opportunity to give elaborative feedback as to why an answer was correct. As the lesson proceeded, I often referred back to the pre-test. During the course of study, I used strategies based on retrieval, spacing, and feedback-driven metacognition. Clicker quizzes were given for spaced practice, usually two days after the initial learning. After all of the lessons had been taught, a chapter exam was given. Here are the average scores my students earned on chapter tests:

Class	CH 4: Ancient Egypt (%)	CH 5: Ancient Mesopotamia (%)	CH 6: Ancient India (%)	CH 8: Ancient Greece (%)	CH 9: Ancient Rome (%)	CH 10: Arabia (%)	CH 13: African Geography (%)	CH 13: Africa (%)
1st Hour	97.01	95.30	91.18	95.42	94.79	96.87	92.59	90.48
2nd Hour	96.15	94.50	94.28	94.12	93.06	96.43	97.44	94.56
4th Hour	95.17	90.20	96.50	94.41	95.56	95.11	95.61	95.49
5th Hour	96.30	95.40	91.25	94.12	94.68	97.08	88.19	92.50
6th Hour	97.09	97.30	97.69	89.71	95.68	96.57	96.15	96.15
7th Hour	91.40	94.60	92.00	87.72	95.96	97.40	97.10	94.82

As stated, I knew my students were thriving; however, I was astounded as I compiled the data that occurred during a 6-month period. The above tables show the data of **over 900 exams**.

What the above scores do not reflect are the projects and essays students completed, because of the subjective nature of grading involved. However, as I graded those more subjectively reviewed assignments, it was clear, because of the interleaving I had also incorporated, that students were both retaining information *and* connecting the dots to deep and critical thinking. I kept data for several years and results were similar; retrieval is ***powerful***.

For those of you who wish to tackle reading research papers, I highly recommend Andrew Watson's gem of a book: *The Goldilocks Map.*[2] I discuss it in almost every presentation I give. He breaks down for us: how to read a research paper, pertinent information to look for, and how not to waste time on papers that don't necessarily apply to us. Andrew Watson can be found in Chapter 8 on Influencers. I have included my review of his book.

Retrieval Time

What are your Retrieval Research Take-aways? Write down your top three.

1. _____

_____

2. _____

_____

3. _____

_____

NOTES

1. Agarwal, Pooja K., and Patrice M. Bain. *Powerful Teaching: Unleash the Science of Learning*. San Francisco: Jossey-Bass, 2019.

2. Watson, Andrew C. *The Goldilocks Map*. Woodbridge: John Catt Publishing, 2021.

Chapter 3

Learning

HOW DO WE LEARN?

It's a question that is as simple as it is profound: "If we don't know how we learn, how can we possibly expect to know how to teach?" The answer lies in understanding the learning process, an essential understanding for any educator aiming to make a real impact in the classroom.[1]

Every year, after the first-quarter grades had been distributed, I had students rush up to me stating, "Mrs. Bain! I have an A (or a B) in your class!" The students would often continue the conversation with, "But I never get good grades." I would notice their slump as they stated, "I always get Ds and Fs." And their tales would end, with them seeming inches shorter, telling me: "I'm not smart." Each time I heard this was like a dagger to my teacher's heart. With determination, my response was always, "But look at you now. The only difference? Now you are learning to learn." It boggles my mind that we have an educational system where students internalize failure by the time they are 11 years old. The good news is that we are surrounded with information, evidence-informed information, based on robust research that allows us to change a failing trajectory for our students. I often felt, especially for my struggling students, that learning was like a giant party, and they simply never received the invitation. It is the very reason I began the first day of every school year stating, "I'm Mrs. Bain. I'm your teacher and I'm going to teach you how to learn."

Daniel Willingham has a wonderful quote in his second edition of *Why Don't Students Like School?*[2] It is:

> Children are more alike than different in terms of how they think and learn.

When I read that, it was as if a lightbulb went off in my head. I read it several times as I thought it to be profound. I interpreted it to mean that whatever the ability level of our students, we can ensure success through using what research tells us about learning. And, furthermore, I found the statement to be true.

Let me begin by giving you a simple answer to a well-researched question: How do we learn? You could immerse yourself in a several-years-long course, diving into research, reading hundreds of books, listening to podcasts, studying articles . . . truly, there is a vast body of research available. In the meantime, I will give you a very basic understanding.

Learning occurs in three steps:

Step 1: Encoding

As teachers, we excel in encoding; it is getting information into our students' heads. Through our various university methods courses and teacher preparation programs, we learn hundreds of ways and strategies to get our curriculum to students.

Step 2: Storage

We teach; the knowledge is stored in our students' heads. Often our teacher programs have ended at this step. Our job is done. Yet, why is it that after a short time, our students have forgotten the very information we worked so hard to teach? In Powerful Teaching,[3] Dr. Agarwal has a quote: "Too often we concentrate on putting information into students' heads. What if, instead, we focused on pulling information out?" This leads us to the crucial third step.

Step 3: Retrieval

Retrieval is the ability to access knowledge, to pull it out. In order for learning to occur, our students must be able to find and bring forth information.

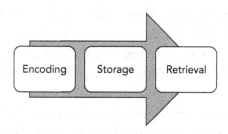

Encoding, storage, and retrieval are the necessary components we need to ensure are available to our students.

I like to use the three-step illustration because it is clear and easy to remember. Although it would be to our great advantage if learning was as linear and straightforward as the arrow, we understand that all learning can be (and often is) messy. Unfortunately, there is often not a clear linear path where we obtain information, store it, and retrieve it when desired. Rather, it often may look more messy.

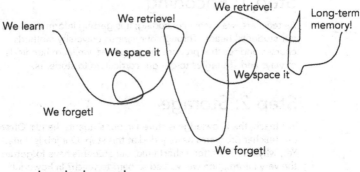

We learn

We retrieve!

We retrieve!

Long-term memory!

We space it

We space it

We forget!

We forget!

Learning is messy!

In the important IES Practice Guide, *Organizing Instruction and Study to Improve Student Learning*,[4] seven research-backed recommendations were given to increase student learning. Although the U.S. Department of Education released this Guide in 2007, these recommendations have withstood the test of time. (In the original Practice Guide, one of the recommendations was referred to as "Testing." This term however, eventually became known as "Retrieval.") As the sole U.S. K–12 practitioner to work on this publication, these ideas helped me look at how we might incorporate them into the research being conducted in my classroom.

There were four recommendations, in particular, that became valuable not only in the research but also key in my teaching repertoire. In the book *Powerful Teaching*, these recommendations are labeled as "Power Tools" because they are the very researched principles that should be in teachers' pedagogical toolboxes.

These four Power Tools are: Retrieval, Spacing, Interleaving, and Feedback-driven Metacognition. In Chapter 4, several strategies will be illustrated and discussed that feature these tools. First, I will share the definitions used from *Powerful Teaching*.

Retrieval

Boosts learning by pulling information out of students' heads rather than cramming information into students' heads. Also known as Retrieval Practice.

Spacing

Revisiting retrieval over time, spreading lessons out over time. Also known as Spaced Practice.

Interleaving

Boosts learning by mixing up closely related topics which encourages discrimination between similarities and differences.

Feedback-driven Metacognition

Boosts learning by providing the opportunity for students to discriminate what they know from what they don't.

Before I discuss the Power Tools in more depth, let me first discuss other aspects of learning that can play a role.

DESIRABLE DIFFICULTY

There is a wonderful line in *Make It Stick*.[5] "Learning that is easy is like writing in sand. Here today and gone tomorrow." How often do our students take delight in completing assignments that require little effort? And how does this contribute to confidence (and possible illusion) that learning has occurred? Robert and Elizabeth Bjork have often been linked to coining the term "Desirable Difficulty," illustrating that learning requires a productive struggle, a challenge. In my classroom, I found that struggling students had an easier time and my above-average students had increased frustration when they were faced with challenging material. I often likened learning and desirable difficulty with the story of the "Three Bears." If learning was too easy, the information wouldn't stick. If learning was too difficult, frustration would result. (And, too often, if this was the case, I would see students simply shut down.) But, when the difficulty was "just right," when there was a productive challenge, learning occurred. I also liked to change the term "desirable difficulty" to Blake Harvard's (https://theeffortfuleducator.com/) paraphrase "*desiring* difficulty." I celebrated desiring difficulties with my students as we knew that learning was happening.

COGNITIVE OVERLOAD

I will begin with more simple definitions. In different parts of our brains, we possess areas for working memory and long-term memory. When we are learning, information first goes to our **working memory,** which is *limited*. In fact, on average, we can take in about 4–7 new items of information. Having too much information coming at us can lead to cognitive overload. If we don't do anything with this information, it is often forgotten. **Long-term memory,** on the other hand, is *unlimited* and our goal is to get information to this area.

Dr. Erika Galea points out:

> Consider, for instance, the role of working memory–the mental workspace where information is temporarily held and manipulated. Educators who know the limitations of short-term memory can organise their lessons to avoid giving students too much information at once, helping prevent them from feeling overwhelmed.
>
> Furthermore, an understanding of long-term memory–the large storage space where knowledge is kept and consolidated–helps educators adopt methods that make it easier for students to remember and find information.[6]

Let's look at familiar scenarios. Have you ever experienced losing your car keys? Not finding your car in the store parking lot? Misplaced items? Chances are your working memory was overloaded and you were experiencing cognitive overload. Or have you been driving to a new destination with no familiar landmarks or known routes? (For me, it requires no talking or music and a heavy reliance on my GPS! By limiting the distractions, I am trying to minimize my cognitive load.) On the other hand, have you ever found yourself in your driveway and realized, "Wait. When did I get off the highway? Why am I suddenly here?" You've most likely taken the route so often that the information is in your long-term memory; you don't have to think about it.

How might cognitive overload impact our students? If students are trying to take notes while the instructor is talking? If math facts haven't been committed to long-term memory? If the classroom is so highly decorated that it causes distractions? Knowing that students can take in 4–7 items of new learning, we can see that cognitive overload can be a real, but solvable, problem.

Let's do an exercise. I'm going to give you a list of letters. Please, give yourself five seconds, take a look at the letters and then, covering the list, write down as many as you can.

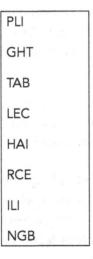

PLI

GHT

TAB

LEC

HAI

RCE

ILI

NGB

How did you do? Were you able to retrieve 4–7 letters? Were you frustrated? Did you experience cognitive overload?

Now let's try the exercise again. This time, however, we will add a strategy called chunking. Chunking is taking new material and linking it with previously known information. I will take the same letters in the same order.

P

LIGHT

TABLE

CHAIR

CEILING

B

I began with the first letter of my first name "P" and ended with the first letter of my last name "B." Now, most likely you would need *less* than the original five seconds and would be able to retrieve all of the letters. Chances are, you were more at ease and did not experience cognitive overload.

If we are bringing new information to our students, one of the best strategies is to "chunk" or link the new information to prior learning. Another gem from Willingham's *Why Don't Students Like School* states:

> Background knowledge allows chunking which makes more room in working memory making it easier to relate to ideas and therefore easier to comprehend.

This simple strategy of linking prior learning to new information decreases cognitive overload, enables us to provide more linked information, and reduces stress and frustration.

The following is a quote by Jill Barshay in her story about how to teach critical thinking:

> And this is where content knowledge becomes important. In order to compare and contrast, the brain has to hold ideas in working memory, which can easily be overloaded. The more familiar a student is with a

particular topic, the easier it is for the student to hold those ideas in his working memory and really think.

This story about how to teach critical thinking was written by Jill Barshay and produced by The Hechinger Report, a nonprofit, independent news organization focused on inequality and innovation in education.[8]

How can you reduce cognitive overload with your students?

DUAL CODING

A picture is worth a thousand words.

Fred R. Barnard

Here is a scenario: You recently purchased a set of shelves and they must be put together. Your preference:

- All instructions are written, no diagrams or illustrations.
- Instructions are intermingled with words and illustrations.

Or perhaps you are listening to a travel podcast and you wish images could be transmitted through the audio waves.

Having images and diagrams available helps us make sense of what we are hearing and seeing. Textbooks use images. Video clips give us images which reflect what we are learning. Sketchnotes can point out important information. Dual coding enables us to give our students a concrete example. It is an important concept and is listed as one of the Seven Recommendations found in *Organizing Instruction and Study to Improve Student Learning:*[9] "Combine graphics with verbal descriptions."

ILLUSIONS OF LEARNING

Illusions of learning can be stumbling blocks and they can be a disconnect with achievement.

You may have had students come up the day of an exam exclaiming, "I'm going to ace this test!" They tell you how they studied for *hours* and feel ready to tackle the test. And, later that evening, as you are grading the exams, you see that one of the students who was *so ready* did not do well at all. Sound familiar? It's really all too common. The student *did* spend a lengthy bit of time preparing; however, the strategies most likely included "looking" over notes, "rereading the chapter," and "seeing what they had highlighted." Because retrieval was not used, students developed a false sense of knowing, known as an **illusion of confidence**. The results are frustrated students, parents ("I saw my child study!"), and the teacher. Ultimately, when a student fails time and time again, after putting in the work, too often the student simply gives up trying. We know how to change this and we owe it to our students to give them the tools to succeed.

Another is an **illusion of fluency**: We *think* we know something but we don't.

For example, what is the capital of the state of New York?

A. Syracuse

B. Albany

C. New York City

D. Rochester

You may think, of course, it's New York City! But the correct answer is Albany. We, and our students, often fall into this trap. The solution, strategies that enable us to discriminate what we know from what we don't. (Hint: Feedback-driven Metacognition! And it's coming next in Chapter 4.)

MEMORY IS THE RESIDUE OF THOUGHT

I am ending this chapter with another quote by Daniel Willingham: "Memory is the residue of thought."[10] I will admit, understanding this did not come readily for me. The meaning became clear when I happened to be thinking about a time when Dr. Agarwal and I were guests on one of Jennifer Gonzalez's Cult of Pedagogy podcasts. Jennifer was discussing how once she taught ancient Greek history, and as a bonus activity, her students made and decorated Greek vases. To her dismay, it turned out her students did not remember much of the ancient Greek history that was taught. Instead, they remembered making the vases. The lightbulb moment occurred; I now knew what Willingham meant. How often, as teachers, do we add that extra story or provide an activity that *takes away* from our teaching? And instead, how can we take a deeper look into tying together stories and projects that reflect learning rather than creating a distraction? If memory is the residue of thought, when our students leave our classrooms, we need to make sure their thinking can reflect learning.

Time for an Elevator Speech . . . Thinking over this chapter. . .

In 30 seconds, what aspects of learning might you tell a fellow teacher?

What are your highlights?

_____

_____

_____

_____

_____

NOTES

1. Galea, E. (2024). Understanding how we think: Why educators need to know how the brain learns. *The Sunday Times of Malta*, 24th March. Available at https://timesofmalta.com/article/understanding-think.1089521 [Accessed 24 March 2024].

2. Willingham, Daniel T. *Why Don't Students Like School?* San Francisco: Jossey-Bass, 2009.

3. Agarwal, Pooja K., and Patrice M. Bain. *Powerful Teaching: Unleash the Science of Learning*. San Francisco: Jossey-Bass, 2019.

4. Pashler, Harold, Patrice M. Bain, Brian A. Bottge, Arthur Graesser, Kenneth Koedinger, Mark McDaniel, and Janet Metcalf. *Organizing Instruction and Study to Improve Student Learning*. Washington, D.C.: National Center for Educational Research, Institute of Education Sciences U.S. Department of Education, 2007. (https://files.eric.ed.gov/fulltext/ED498555.pdf)

5. Brown, Peter C., Henry L. Roediger, and Mark A. McDaniel. *Make It Stick: The Science of Successful Learning*. Cambridge, MA: Harvard University Press, 2014.

6. Galea, Erika. Understanding how we think: Why educators need to know how the brain learns. *The Sunday Times of Malta*, 24th March, 2024. Available at https://timesofmalta.com/article/understanding-think.1089521 [Accessed 24 March 2024].

7. Willingham, Daniel T. *Why Don't Students Like School?* San Francisco: Jossey-Bass, 2009.

8. Barshay, Jill. Scientific research on how to teach critical thinking contradicts education trends. *The Hechinger Report*, 9 September 2019. Available at: https://hechingerreport.org/scientific-research-on-how-to-teach-critical-thinking-contradicts-education-trends/ [Accessed 12 May 2024].

9. Pashler, Harold, Patrice M. Bain, Brian A. Bottge, Arthur Graesser, Kenneth Koedinger, Mark McDaniel, and Janet Metcalf. *Organizing Instruction and Study to Improve Student Learning.* Washington, D.C.: National Center for Educational Research, Institute of Education Sciences U.S. Department of Education, 2007. (https://files.eric.ed.gov/fulltext/ED498555.pdf)

10. Willingham, Daniel. Ask the Cognitive Scientist: What will improve a student's memory? *American Educator,* Winter 2008–2009. Available at https://www.aft.org/sites/default/files/willingham_0.pdf [Accessed 24 April 2024].

Chapter 4

Power Tools

When educators use evidence-based practices in their teaching methodology, they can help students learn more deeply and gain knowledge and skills that last a lifetime.[1]

Dr. Erika Galea

While writing *Powerful Teaching*, Dr. Agarwal and I coined the term "Power Tools," those researched principles that have been shown to increase learning and knowledge retention. These Power Tools are: retrieval, spacing, interleaving, and feedback-driven metacognition. There are many reasons why they should be included in every teacher's toolbox.

- They are not based on fads or myths. I cannot tell you how many *years* I sat through professional development that was based on "the latest thing" and did nothing to increase my pedagogical skills or my students' learning. I was often required to include these practices in my teaching, and administrators included the use of them in my evaluations. What's more, each year, it was another fad and the cycle continued. The Power Tools are based on robust research that has been replicated many times.

- Power Tools can be used for most ages and content. I have used them with children in preschool, primary, middle, and high schools, and college students. I have used them in training with teachers, administrators, parents, and even people in business and police officers.

- You may already be using them as those intuitive skills that good teachers simply know work. Power Tools, however, take us a step beyond intuition. They give us a shared language and remind us to be intentional and purposeful and explain why they are necessary for learning.

- Often, making a small change can lead to a big difference. For example, rather than beginning a class by stating, "Remember, yesterday we discussed. . ." (which is encoding) your opening words can easily be changed to "What did we discuss yesterday? Turn and talk with your neighbor." By following this with a group share, you have created a room rich with retrieval within 90 seconds.

POWER TOOL #1: RETRIEVAL

We retrieve information all of the time. In fact, take a moment and reflect upon these questions:

- What is a story of family lore you remember from your childhood?

- What was your best vacation ever?

- What is an odor you hope to never smell again?

For the most part, we enjoy bringing forth memories of vacations, nights out with friends, our children's toddling years, family lore . . . some people (like me!) even relish attending trivia nights. Retrieval can be a rewarding experience.

Yet, why is it that our students often are riddled with stress and anxiety as they approach tests and exams? Actually, we know why. We know that when retrieval is infrequent and used for high-stakes exams, students often feel unprepared and anxious and may spend hours cramming for those exams. In my school district, as discussed in *Powerful Teaching*,[2] 1,500 high-school students (who had been using retrieval throughout the course of study) were asked: "Does using retrieval make you more or less anxious for unit tests?" The results are given in a pie chart.[3]

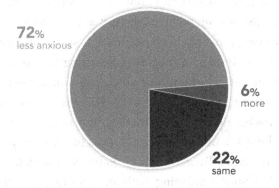

72% less anxious

6% more

22% same

Why did over 1,500 high school students report this? Because when retrieval is used throughout the course of study, students are *prepared*. They have had ample opportunities to ensure they know the material before they are in high-stakes situations. And, personally, I witnessed this decreased stress and anxiety year after year with my students. In fact, I simply stopped using the word "tests" with my students; instead, they were called "celebrations" because it was truly a celebration both for my students and for me to witness how much they had learned.

Let's get to retrieval basics.

I defined retrieval by saying that it: boosts learning by pulling information out of students' heads rather than cramming information into students' heads.

For learning to happen, information must first be encoded. We must get the information *into* our heads before we can retrieve or access that information. To help this learning stick, it is best to link new information with what has previously been learned. As we retrieve information, research has shown that learning is actually strengthened.[4]

There are various methods and strategies to encourage retrieval. What is most beneficial is when low or no stakes, meaning few or no points, are awarded (or taken off) when retrieval strategies are used. It certainly does not mean that grading is discontinued. Rather, low- or no-stakes retrieval is used from the time learning begins and continues throughout the course of the chapter or unit, whereas the test at the conclusion of the chapter or unit most likely results in high-stakes grading. I like to think of retrieval as a train trip. Learning begins at the station and ends at a destination (which could be thought of as a high-stakes test, project, essay, etc.). However, all of the stops the train makes along the way are the opportunities for retrieval and checking for understanding. Opportunities vary and can be as simple as a "Turn and Talk," Retrieval Cards (see Chapters 6 and 7), and/or quizzing, with many strategies in-between. The good news is that you may already be using many retrieval strategies. My goal with this book is to give you strategies and background so that your use is intentional and purposeful.

Retrieval Is a Learning Strategy, Not an Assessment Strategy

Sometimes we are under the illusion that just because we see something (perhaps, many times!), we know it. However, simply *seeing* something doesn't mean we know it. Let's do an exercise.

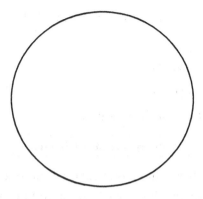

Think of a coin you have seen from childhood to now. Sketch it. The coin may include a person. Which way does the person face? What is the person wearing? Is there a structure on the coin? What writing is found on the coin? Is there a date? Where is the date located? You may have seen this coin *hundreds* of times, you definitely know it when you see it, but can you *retrieve it*?

Try another one. How often have you seen the "Apple" logo? Drawing it should be easy, right? It's an apple! Go ahead and sketch it.

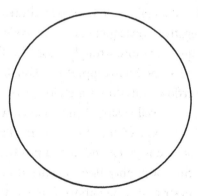

Compare your sketches to a coin or the real Apple logo. How did you do? And why did I ask you to make these drawings? To make the point: Just because we *see* something does not mean we *know* it. Think for a moment what we often ask our students to do:

- **Reread** the chapter.
- **Look** at what you highlighted.
- **See** what you wrote in your notes.

> "Seeing" is not retrieving.

We, as teachers, know our curriculum and our students. We can look to previous years and ascertain what has been taught to our students. As stated earlier from the book *Make It Stick*, it is best to link new information with previously learned material. I will give you two examples of how I did this in my classroom.

- I used pre-tests before every lesson, offering elaborative feedback after each question. Doing this helped to activate prior knowledge. Because I knew my students well, I made sure to explain the concept and tie it in with something I had previously taught or found in their life experiences.
- Specifically, when I taught the ancient river civilizations, flooding played a major role in those cultures, and had positive and negative consequences. To encode knowledge of these consequences more strongly, I used local examples. We live very close to the Mississippi River. Usually in the spring, the river overflows and floods a major piece of nearby land. The students are well aware of the area. However, often the students didn't connect the dots that in the summer that same piece of land is green and lush: a positive consequence. At another time, a mighty flood occurred near our district and totally destroyed a neighboring town; the entire town had to move to higher ground: a negative consequence.

Simply spending a few minutes activating this prior knowledge helped the students understand the consequences the people of ancient civilizations faced.

Time to Ponder. . .

Think of your curriculum . . . How can you link prior learning to new material?

In Chapter 2 on research, I discussed the "pop final" we gave to determine how much my students remembered without advance notice or opportunities to study. I have included a reminder of the graph.

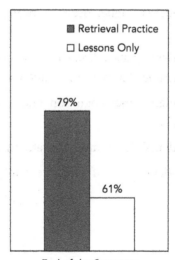

■ Retrieval Practice
□ Lessons Only

79%

61%

End of the Semester

I thought the results were quite interesting and confirmed the hypothesis that retrieval works. However, as I looked at the individual scores, a red flag emerged which led to a summer of pondering. My number-one student, the one who had gotten 100% on every piece of homework and test, scored in the less than 50th percentile on this final exam. How was it possible? I realized that my homework did not include retrieval and my prediction was that this particular student crammed before exams, which often leads to high scores and quick forgetting. My summer of pondering led me to devising many strategies you will find in Chapter 6.

We know retrieval has many benefits. A paper adapted by Roediger, Putnam, and Smith[5] listed ten benefits. I was going to choose my top five; however, I witnessed all ten in my classroom and so I am including all. Retrieval

1. improves students' learning and retention of information over the long term.

2. increases students' higher-order thinking and transfer of knowledge.

3. identifies students' gaps in knowledge, which provides formative assessment for teachers and students.

4. increases students' metacognition and awareness of their own learning.

5. increases students' engagement and attention in class.

6. increases students' use of effective study strategies outside of class.

7. increases students' advance preparation for class.

8. improves students' mental organization of knowledge.

9. increases students' learning of related information that isn't initially retrieved.

10. increases students' learning in the future by blocking interfering information.

To achieve these benefits, it is important to ensure that retrieval strategies include simple recall and higher-order skills. If we want students to think on a higher level, we should make sure our retrieval questions include both types of questions. In a study done at my school with 8th-grade science students (age 14–15), students were given retrieval opportunities with both fact and application questions. Retrieval of the application questions resulted in the biggest boost in performance on the final exam with complex questions (Agarwal and Bain, p. 41).[6] As part of Pooja Agarwal's dissertation, she conducted an experiment that used a mix of basic concept questions and higher-order questions. She found that the mix of these two types of retrieval produced the highest exam performance, higher than basic questions alone.[7]

After *Powerful Teaching* was released, Dr. Agarwal and I received a wonderful gift from the very talented Mary Kemper.[8] She had created sketchnotes based on our book. Mary has graciously given me her permission to use them throughout the book. Take a look at the graphic and ponder. What looks familiar? What looks new?

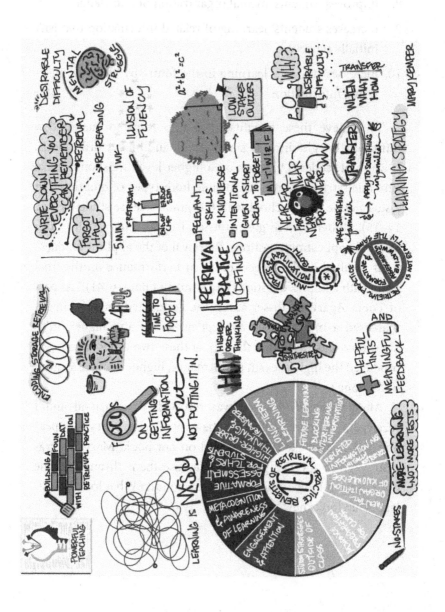

I have an activity for you (and, yes, it includes Retrieval!). The activity is a strategy called Think and Link.

Retrieval Practice
Think and Link

Based on a strategy by Kate Jones

Without looking back, complete this form.

1. Recall what you learned from reading about retrieval and learning.

2. Recall what you saw in the sketchnote.

3. Apply and synthesize the two to create a deeper level of understanding.

What do you recall about retrieval and learning?	What do you recall about the sketchnote?

Name 4 things you can retrieve about learning:

1. _____

2. _____

3. _____

4. _____

POWER TOOL # 2: SPACING

"High test scores reflect learning." It may surprise you, but that sentence is debated by cognitive scientists and educators. For example, if one "crams" the night before an exam, one is likely to obtain a high grade on a final exam. However, asking the student to discuss items one month later often reflects that actual learning did not occur.

Forgetting is good for learning. This statement seems so counterintuitive. However, it is true. As stated earlier, retrieval strengthens memory. Research has shown that when we learn something, chances are we can retrieve it soon after it has been learned. Yet, if we wait too long before the information is retrieved, at times, it is as if we didn't learn it at all. (Think how often the first several weeks of school are spent reviewing and reteaching the material from a previous year.) What best promotes and strengthens learning is when we have forgotten information just a bit; that feeling of having something on the tip of our tongue while we look up at the ceiling as if the answer could be pulled down from above. It is when we retrieve at *that* point that learning is strengthened. Waiting for that point of forgetting and then succeeding in retrieval, is spaced practice. Research discussing this type of forgetting and spaced retrieval dates back to the 1880s with studies conducted by Hermann Ebbinghaus and is often referred to as the "Forgetting Curve." To give a brief description, Ebbinghaus concluded that we begin forgetting as soon as we finish going over material. In order to retain knowledge, we need to space out retrieval: Retrieve the information the next day and again a few days later. We should then follow this by adding more time between retrieval opportunities with the goal of getting this information into long-term memory.

As teachers, we work incredibly hard and put in many long hours bringing forth learning to our students. It can be incredibly

Doug Lemov's Annotated Forgetting Curve

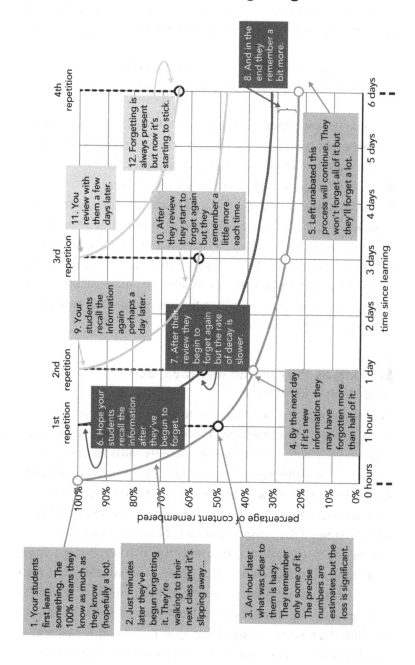

1. Your students first learn something. The 100% means they know as much as they know (hopefully a lot).

2. Just minutes later they've begun forgetting it. They're walking to their next class and it's slipping away...

3. An hour later what was clear to them is hazy. They remember only some of it. The precise numbers are estimates but the loss is significant.

4. By the next day if it's new information they may have forgotten more than half of it.

5. Left unabated this process will continue. They won't forget all of it but they'll forget a lot.

6. Hope your students recall the information after they've begun to forget.

7. After their review they begin to forget again but the rate of decay is slower.

8. And in the end they remember a bit more.

9. Your students recall the information again perhaps a day later.

10. After they review they start to forget again but they remember a little more each time.

11. You review with them a few days later.

12. Forgetting is always present but now it's starting to stick.

frustrating to realize that forgetting is part of the process. However, we now know how to turn forgetting into strategies that will strengthen learning. As Emma Turner states in her book *Initium*,

> Recognise that forgetting is inevitable; believing we are powerless to mitigate for its effects is not.[9]

Doug Lemov, author of the great book *Teach Like a Champion*,[10] has one of the most detailed infographics that best helps teachers.

We learn, we forget. We retrieve, we space, and we retrieve again. It is this process that aids long-term learning.

We can look at spacing, or spaced practice, in two ways. First, spacing can be defined as purposeful retrieval at intentional intervals. Second, it can mean spacing out the teaching of a unit's information over time. For example, rather than an intense focus on a subject and moving on, learning will be more robust if it is spread out. In addition, allowing for some forgetting makes for the most powerful learning.

Spacing as Purposeful Retrieval at Intentional Intervals

Let's begin with the definition of purposeful retrieval at intentional intervals. If something is taught and *not* revisited until a high-stakes exam, unfortunately, students must basically start from scratch as the big test approaches. They may have learned it initially, but it is gone. And, if something had been taught *and retrieved days later – but not again,* it does not indicate *long-term* learning if the information hadn't been revisited throughout the course of study. It is that revisiting that is called spacing.

There are several studies that show how students can lose over half of the information that had been taught if it hadn't been spaced. Cognitive scientists Doug Rohrer and Kelli Taylor conducted a research study[11] looking at cramming versus spacing. What they found was that students initially scored higher when cramming was used. However, when tested on the material after four weeks, the scores of the students who had crammed had drastically dropped. (I can attest to this from my own college days!) The graph illustrates their findings.

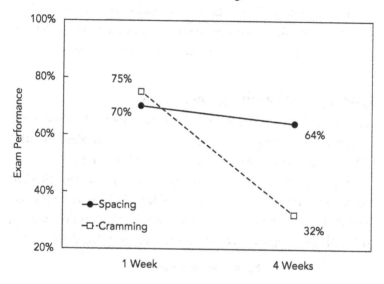

Many studies reach similar conclusions. As we discussed in *Powerful Teaching*,[12] "What's good for learning in the short term, like rereading and cramming, leads to a huge drop-off in learning over the long term when compared to challenging strategies like retrieval practice and spacing."[13]

A question I am often asked: With *so much* on my teaching plate, how can I find the time to keep going back to retrieve previously learned information? I know that overwhelming feeling. Yet, what I learned from the research was that using the strategies that promote learning leads to more effective and efficient teaching and reduces the time spent on reviews. I also learned how to gauge what needed to be spaced. We can't space everything or we would never be able to move on. I became selective and began by looking at what I called my "Big Ticket" items: items on tests, information needed for essays or projects, what students need to know for the following term . . . and those are the items I would space.

Think back to where I compared learning to a train ride. The station was the beginning of the unit and the destination was the end, defined by high-stakes tests and exams. I stated all of the stops along the route were opportunities for retrieval: This is spacing – the purposeful retrieval at intentional intervals.

Spacing Out Teaching Over Time

Too often, units are taught as a "one and done." Textbooks are written to cover important topics in a unit, complete the unit with an exam, and move on to the next unit, and repeat.

After *Organizing Instruction and Study to Improve Student Learning*[14] was released, the Doing What Works website https://dwwlibrary.wested.org/ produced several infographics, videos, and audio recordings related to the IES Practice Guide.

Space learning over time

Look at the slide from a Regional Educational Lab (REL) Mid-Atlantic for a Common Ground Bridge Event I led. The information, from the Doing What Works library, illustrates an example of spacing out teaching over time. Also, listen to Mark McDaniel explain the concepts of spacing learning over time at https://dwwlibrary.wested.org/resources/624.

Classroom Research

Study done in Science at Columbia Middle School

Control Group

Traditionally, mitosis taught in one class period:
Students read material, learned terms

In the CMS Study, the SAME AMOUNT OF TIME was spent on mitosis.

Experimental Group

However, rather than using one class period,
it was divided and put with other topics

DOINGWHATW♦RKS
research-based education practices online

Three weeks after the presentation of material, students showed a **50%** increase on

- answering questions about specific terms.
- generating fill-in-the-blank answers.
- writing essays describing mitosis.
- illustrating the process of mitosis.

Blake Harvard wrote an article called: "Assuming – Enemy of the Effective Classroom."[15]

Blake captured important points in this article that relate to retrieval and spacing.

> Over a century of evidence points to two study methods that cast a wide net with respect to accessibility of use and positive impact on differing learners: **retrieval practice and spaced practice.** These learning strategies provide for more efficient and effective studying while also informing students of their level of understanding. Learning is effortful. Studying is effortful. By distributing

their study sessions and attempting to recall or recognize information (rather than just reread about it), students are participating in a more impactful practice. And these are study habits that will benefit our students from elementary school through college. When employed properly they take the assuming out of studying. Students know what they know and they know what they don't know. Then, that information is used to drive their future spaced study sessions on the material.

Because retrieval and spacing go hand in hand, you will find many strategies in Chapters 6 and 7 that you may find useful for your students.

POWER TOOL #3: INTERLEAVING

Too often, retrieval gets a bad reputation as some might say it is the simple regurgitation of facts. My response is that factual knowledge is the necessary first step. However, an injustice is served if we stop at that base level. We strive for deep and critical thinking and one of the ways to achieve that is through interleaving.

I define interleaving as comparing and contrasting similar content. Doing so improves discrimination and critical thinking.

I once had a science teacher ask me, "So, if I compare chemistry and biology, is that interleaving?" No, it isn't. We used an example such as this in *Powerful Teaching*:[16] Think of interleaving as making a fruit salad. You may put in bananas, apples, oranges, grapes, strawberries . . . but you wouldn't add in a tomato, even though it is a fruit. In interleaving, content must be similar.

Often, interleaving is thought of within a mathematical framework and a typical assignment (using what is known as blocking rather than interleaving) could be: Solve the following five addition problems and five subtraction problems.

To apply interleaving, you want to switch up the problems. This enables students to really think about what is being asked. The problems are mixed up together.

To help further clarify, Brown, Roediger, and McDaniel in *Make It Stick*[17] use a great analogy and I will paraphrase. Let's say you are a baseball or softball coach and you are at practice. The pitcher might throw 10 fast balls, 10 slow balls, 10 curve balls . . . and the batter always knows what is coming. However, if you instruct the pitcher to *interleave*, or switch up the throws (perhaps a fast, curve, 2 slows, 1 curve, 2 fasts. . .), from the time the ball leaves the pitcher's hand, the batter must think (and quickly!) all he or she knows about hitting the ball and utilize that information to make the best possible hit. *That* is what we want in our classrooms; we don't want our students to automatically know what is coming. We want them to take all they know about a subject and inter*weave* the facts to create critical thinking.

The performance effects of blocking and interleaving are shown in a graph of a study done by Taylor and Rohrer.[18] In a nutshell, 4th-grade students (approximately age 9–10) were given math problems on prisms and faces. Some of the students were given problems that were blocked (all prisms followed by all faces); others were given problems that were interleaved (both types of problems). A quiz was given at the end of the class and again the following day. One of the best ways to ensure a high grade is to quiz immediately after learning information. And, this is precisely what happened with the blocked group. They knew what was coming and aced the quiz. However, the students who had the interleaved problems, at the end of class, struggled a bit. What happened at the quiz the following day? The forgetting curve proved to be true; however, look how much more information the interleaved group had retained.

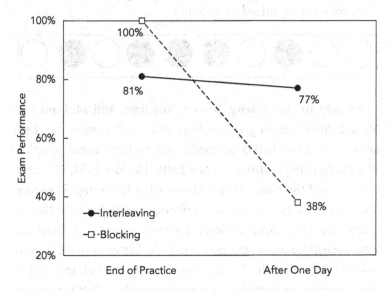

Although most studies of interleaving are used within mathematics, does interleaving work for other subjects as well? I know for a fact it does, I used it in my classroom. However, I needed to take the textbook material that had been blocked and create my own interleaving. Here is an example from my World History class: The textbook had a unit on revolutions, a lesson each on: Industrial, French, and Russian.

Once the information had been taught, the book moved on to the next revolution followed by the next. It was clearly blocked and there was no comparison or contrasting of information. To create interleaving, I developed Essential Questions. To do this, I created a common question pertaining to all of the revolutions. At the beginning of the unit, I wrote the question on the front board and referred to it daily. My Essential Question for this particular unit was: How did the lives of the working people change as a result of the revolution? In a different year, my question was:

How did social pyramids change as a result of the revolutions? Students learned the facts of each but, with the Essential Question, were able to compare and contrast, promoting critical thinking and deep learning as they wove together the facts around the question. At the conclusion of the unit, included on the exam, was an essay based upon the Essential Question.

I often think that teachers have opportunities to be great choreographers when it comes to interleaving. I like to think of it as a wonderful dance, intentionally weaving important questions (and discussions) through the lessons at just the right moment. Inter*weave* to inter*leave*!

Mary Kemper's sketchnote on spacing and interleaving illustrates this very well.

Two Things

What are two things in the sketchnote (following page) that helped you make a connection with spacing and/or interleaving?

1. _____

2. _____

POWER TOOL #4: FEEDBACK-DRIVEN METACOGNITION

Feedback-driven metacognition might be my favorite Power Tool. As stated, I began teaching my students how to learn on the first day of school, and it started with metacognition. A simple question I asked was: Did you ever study hard for a test and not do well? Consistently, year after year, the majority of student hands waved through the air and the nickname "Mrs. Metacognition" was often given to me.

Let's try an exercise. Who was Lady Murasaki Shikibu? Chances are you either knew the answer or you didn't. And

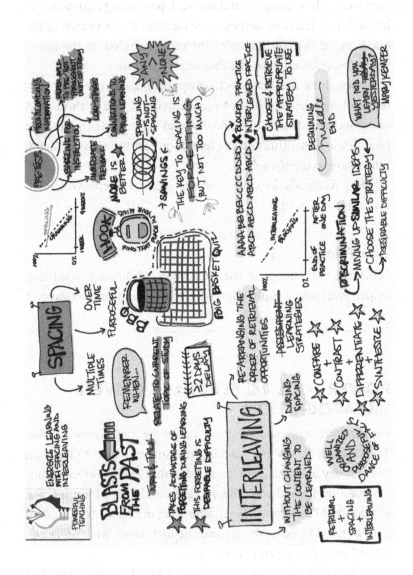

furthermore, you *knew* if you didn't know it! This is an example of metacognition: discriminating what we know from what we don't. (Lady Murasaki Shikibu was a Japanese princess who lived around the year 1000. She is often credited with writing the world's first novel: *The Tale of Genji*.)

Too often, students aren't given the opportunity for this discrimination until a high-stakes exam occurs. Like retrieval and spacing, strategies illustrating metacognition should be used throughout the course of study. In Chapter 3, I discussed the illusion of confidence: I'm going to ace the test! But they don't. Students tend to study what they already know because it builds their confidence and skip over what they don't know because it is a struggle. Utilizing strategies based in metacognition allows students to make that differentiation and concentrate study on what they don't know, making for a more efficient and effective study.

One of the keys is ensuring that feedback is given so students can ascertain what they know and what requires further study. We sometimes think that feedback is only valuable for incorrect responses. However, feedback should be given any time we ask our students to retrieve. Why? Sometimes students guess; they get the correct answer but don't know why. In addition, the feedback can validate that students are on the right path and it helps put an end to illusions.

Look at the example of a research study done in a 7th-grade (age 12–13) science class. We can see that some of the chapter material was not retrieved (quizzed), and some of the information was retrieved with no feedback (this could mean checkmarks for incorrect answers, a percentage grade at the top of the paper, etc.). The third group took a retrieval quiz and received elaborative feedback as to why the answer was correct. Does feedback matter?

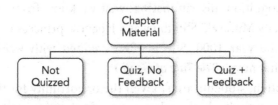

7th Grade Science

Exam after ~18 days

Agarwal, Roediger, McDanial, and McDermott (2009)

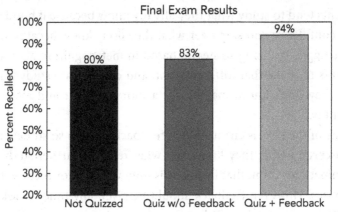

Final Exam Results

Agarwal, Roediger, McDanial, and McDermott (2009)

Once again, we see that retrieval is better than no retrieval. However, look at the difference in the scores simply by adding feedback as to why answers were correct!

I would like to take a moment to discuss errors. I had a large sign that was front and center in my classroom:

It's okay to make mistakes; that's the way we learn.

I did not see errors as problems; rather, they were similar to a map showing that a different direction was needed. Students were therefore not threatened by errors and when they occurred during the course of study, students were able to attend to those areas which required additional study. This is another reason why offering low- and no-stakes opportunities during the learning phase is important. Students did not spend additional time on what they already knew; rather they concentrated on what still needed to be learned. The result? When the time came for the high-stakes exams, my students were ready. Using metacognition and evidence-informed strategies assists students to soar.

I've shared research on the Power Tools in Chapter 3; I would like to share a couple of my favorite firsthand accounts that illustrate how incorporating the tools, with my 11-year-old students, leads to long-term learning:

- It was quite common for former students, who were now in college, to email me detailing their excitement when a professor brought up a subject and their minds flooded with information they had learned in my class.

- I received an email from a parent after the family took a summer vacation in Europe. (I had had the daughters in my class five years earlier.) The mother was astonished by the facts and stories the girls told the parents at each historical site. Each time, the girls were asked how they already knew the information. Their reply: "Oh, we learned that in Mrs. Bain's class!"

- One year I randomly ran into two former students that I hadn't seen in six years. As soon as they saw me, they began rattling off facts and stories from their time in my class. It went on for several minutes; I felt like I was at a ping pong match watching their volley of facts.

We want our students to retain knowledge. We want them to be able to access previously learned information. The use of Power Tools enables these wants to become a reality.

In Chapters 6 and 7, you will find strategies I created based on retrieval, spacing, and feedback-driven metacognition.

Following is the Mary Kemper sketchnote on Metacognition.

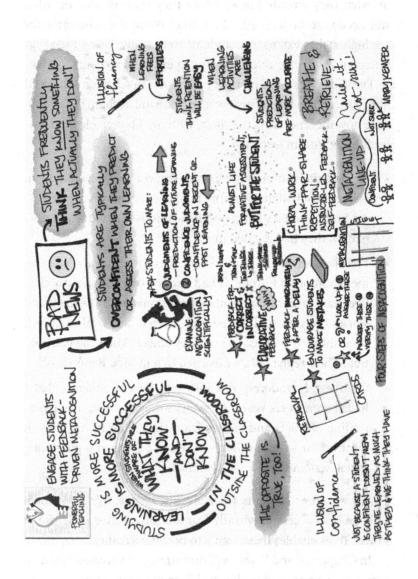

Now it's your turn! How would you create your own sketchnote for Power Tools?

NOTES

1. Galea, Erika. Understanding how we think: Why educators need to know how the brain learns. *The Sunday Times of Malta*, 24 March 2024. Available at https://timesofmalta.com/article/understanding-think.1089521 [Accessed 24 March 2024].

2. Agarwal, Pooja K., and Patrice M. Bain. *Powerful Teaching: Unleash the Science of Learning.* San Francisco: Jossey-Bass, 2019.

3. Agarwal, Pooja K., et al. Classroom-based programs of retrieval practice reduce middle and high school students' test anxiety. *Journal of Applied Research in Memory and Cognition* 3: 131–139, 2014.

4. Brown, Peter C., Henry L. Roediger, and Mark A. McDaniel. *Make It Stick: The Science of Successful Learning.* Cambridge, MA: Harvard University Press, 2014.

5. The list of ten benefits of retrieval practice is adapted from Roediger, Henry L., Adam L. Putnam, and Megan A. Smith. Ten benefits of testing and their applications to educational practice. In *Psychology of Learning and Motivation: Cognition in Education* (eds. Jose Mestre and Brian Ross), 1–36. Oxford: Elsevier, 2011.

6. Agarwal, Pooja K., and Patrice M. Bain. *Powerful Teaching: Unleash the Science of Learning.* San Francisco: Jossey-Bass, 2019.

7. Agarwal, Pooja K. Retrieval practice and Bloom's taxonomy: Do students need fact knowledge before higher order learning? *Journal of Educational Psychology* 11: 189–209, 2019.

8. Mary Kemper serves as Executive Director for Instructional Leadership in Coppell ISD in Coppell, TX. She can be contacted at: mkemper@coppellisd.com.

9. Turner, Emma. *Initium: Cognitive Science and Research-informed Primary Practice.* John Catt from Hodder Education, 2023.

10. Lemov, Doug. *Teach Like a Champion 3.0.* San Francisco: Jossey-Bass, 2021. Available at: https://teachlikeachampion.com/blog/an-annotated-forgetting-curve/ [Accessed 12 May 2024].

11. Rohrer, Doug, and Kelli Taylor. The effects of overlearning and distributed practice on the retention of mathematics knowledge. *Applied Cognitive Psychology* 20: 1209–1224, 2006.

12. Agarwal, Pooja K., and Patrice M. Bain. *Powerful Teaching: Unleash the Science of Learning.* San Francisco: Jossey-Bass, 2019.

13. Maddox, Geoffrey B. Understanding the underlying mechanism of the spacing effect in verbal learning: A case for encoding variability and study-phase retrieval. *Journal of Cognitive Psychology* 28: 684–706, 2016.

14. Pashler, Harold, Patrice M. Bain, Brian A. Bottge, Arthur Graesser, Kenneth Koedinger, Mark McDaniel, and Janet Metcalf. *Organizing Instruction and Study to Improve Student Learning.* Washington, D.C.: National Center for Educational Research, Institute of Education Sciences U.S. Department of Education, 2007. (https://files.eric.ed.gov/fulltext/ED498555.pdf)

15. Harvard, Blake. Assuming – Enemy of the effective. *The Effortful Educator*, 29 March 2022. Available at: https://theeffortfuleducator.com/2022/03/29/assuming/) [Accessed 12 May 2024].

16. Agarwal, Pooja K., and Patrice M. Bain. *Powerful Teaching: Unleash the Science of Learning.* San Francisco: Jossey-Bass, 2019.

17. Brown, Peter C., Henry L. Roediger, and Mark A. McDaniel. *Make It Stick: The Science of Successful Learning.* Cambridge, MA: Harvard University Press, 2014.

18. Taylor, Kelli, and Doug Rohrer. The effects of interleaved practice. *Applied Cognitive Psychology* 24: 837–848, 2010.

Chapter **5**

Schools and Conferences

SCHOOLS

I began giving workshops to teachers and administrators in 2008. These started out locally, then expanded throughout my area and eventually led to national and international workshops, presentations, webinars, and podcasts.

I have been fortunate to work with many schools; I would like to highlight a couple of them that were so very memorable for me.

The first workshop came less than a month after the book launch (2019) of *Powerful Teaching*. Dr. Agarwal was working at the Berklee College of Music in Boston, Massachusetts, and it was a joy to have our first *Powerful Teaching* presentation together at **Carl Sandburg High School** outside of Chicago, Illinois.

My first solo *Powerful Teaching* presentation was at **St. Vrain Valley School District** in Longmont, Colorado, later that year.

I was absolutely impressed with the leaders and faculty. They had conducted a *Powerful Teaching* Book Study and each person of this cohort chose a section of the book and became an "expert" on that section. Each person had created a large tri-fold display with research, and these were on display through a long corridor, with my presentation in the auditorium at one end of the corridor and the food at the other! As teachers left my presentations, each expert was available at their display to answer questions. I thought this was brilliant on so many levels; as the school year went on, other schools would host Book Studies, and each school already had an expert on hand. The people who were instrumental in bringing me to St. Vrain were administrators **Diane Lauer** and **Kim Wiggins**. I thought Dr. Wiggins's approach to conducting the book studies and encouraging teacher experts was superb. In subsequent training to other schools, I frequently called it the "Wiggins Model." I have been following the incredible work of St. Vrain since 2019. In five years, they have created professional development around the science of learning that is top-notch. You will find resources which can show you some of St. Vrain's strategies in Chapter 7: Teachers and Leaders.

In addition, there were also two teachers of St. Vrain who gave me the inspiration to write this book! Over the years, I have been frequently tagged on social media by people who have used my strategies, adapted my strategies, or created new strategies. In the summer of 2023, **Suzannah Evans** tagged me with a photo of teachers engaging with the science of learning. My first reaction was to bookmark the photos. This led me to think about all of the other strategies I have bookmarked, saved . . . and to the realization that there needed to be ONE PLACE where I could locate the information I had been saving for years. While I began compiling, I thought, "Perhaps others would find this useful as well!" and the writing of this book began. Thank you, Suzy! Together with Suzy, I was a guest on the "Vrain Waves" podcast with **Shane Saeed**, another St. Vrain leader. Minutes before the podcast, I told them how they had inspired me to write this book. We were all giddy with excitement while keeping the book a secret.

I flew to San Francisco, California, in the latter part of February 2020; **Danielle Devencenzi** had invited me to work with the faculty at the **St. Ignatius College Preparatory School**. In addition to working with a talented and knowledgeable staff, it was my first time visiting San Francisco. Leaving the snowy Midwest to visit the beautiful greenery of California was a dream. Little did I know that within two weeks, everyone and everywhere would shut down due to COVID-19. My presentations turned virtual as I grasped the memory of being able to be present and in-person with the faculty of St. Ignatius.

Life changed during the COVID-19 pandemic. My presentations became virtual. Like most teachers, I struggled with not seeing faces, nor eyes during "aha" moments; I was no longer able to conduct a quick Turn and Talk, or hear the giggling at one of my stories. While we were all locked down, I had a particular presentation that was eventful. The school shall remain nameless. This school had a large faculty and learning was remote. Each participant's computer camera was off. In the midst of my presentation, foul language began to sprawl across the screen and I was unable to erase it. It turned out the teacher had left the presentation and her adolescent son got on her computer, displaying the words. After a small bit of time had passed, I simply said, "Okay, time to erase that now," which he did. One of my favorite comments from after the presentation: "You can tell Patrice taught middle school. She went right on teaching without missing a beat!"

One of my favorite moments was while I was presenting to the faculty at **Katz Yeshiva High School** in Boca Raton, Florida, having been invited by **Rabbi Avi Wasser**. During the lunch break between my morning and afternoon sessions, I witnessed a beautiful ceremony. The school was presented with a new, hand-lettered Torah. How rare to be given the opportunity to witness something so meaningful to all in attendance.

In 2022, I had the privilege of working with the faculty at **Frederick County Public Schools** (FCPS) in Frederick, Maryland, at the invitation of **Margaret (Meg) Lee**. I first met some of the FCPS faculty and leaders, including Meg, at a researchED conference in Philadelphia, Pennsylvania, in 2019 and we became mutual followers. FCPS has embraced the science of learning. They bring in world-renowned experts and evidence-informed learning and strategies are woven into the FCPS fabric for all to wear and share. They have set a high bar for all of us to follow.

If you want to see how the science of learning is, and should be, embedded in a school, I highly recommend the following schools (in alphabetical order so as to not show favoritism!):

- Delta County Public Schools, Delta, Colorado (https://www.deltaschools.com)
- Frederick County Public Schools, Frederick, Maryland (https://www.fcps.org)
- St. Andrew's Episcopal School, Potomac, Maryland (https://www.saes.org/)
- St. Vrain Valley School District, Longmont, Colorado (https://www.svvsd.org/)

I would like to give a shout-out to two people whom I have had the honor and privilege to work with and bring *Powerful Teaching* to their respective teachers and schools:

- **Carol Pfleiderer,** who brought evidence-informed teaching and strategies to teachers in **Ethiopia** (thank you Christy Crary for the connection).
- **Assiya Zhanabay,** who brought *Powerful Teaching* to teachers in **Kazakhstan**.

It is mind-boggling for me to realize that teachers around the globe are embracing the science of learning and the research that began in my classroom.

My favorite comment I ever received was while I was giving a presentation to a Trust of teachers in England upon an invitation from Cheryl Lott. After the presentation was over, one of the participants said to Cheryl while referring to me, "I wish she was my mum!"

The last school I would like to highlight is the **Eudora School District** in Eudora, Kansas (https://www.eudoraschools.org/). I was invited to speak there in January 2023 by **Heather Hundley**. As always, I am honored to be invited to speak to faculty. And there are times that I want to take what I see and share it with others. Here are three cases in point. I was the invited speaker for their "Dream Big Conference," an event bringing teachers back after a holiday break. It *was* a celebration! Not your typical staff meetings but a day of research-worthy professional development delivering strategies to the teachers. The energy was contagious. And one of my favorite parts is that the professional development was not only attended by teachers. The *administrators* and *school board members* also took part. I witnessed school board members interacting with staff, discussing students, strategies . . . I felt such a sense of unity. Another of my favorite parts was the catered lunch. It was not an outside caterer; rather, all school events are catered by high-school students as part of their hospitality and cooking classes. I thought it was brilliant. Students were getting actual experience in catering: what is involved, what is needed, and how to cook and bake for large crowds (and the food was outstanding!). And finally, Ms. Hundley had asked if I would conduct a session for parents the prior evening – again, attended by school board members along with parents. I wanted to end my highlights with Eudora because what I felt, as a guest at their school, was a cohesion and commitment we should all aspire to. As a thank-you gift, Ms. Hundley gave me a mug that I now use every day. The message empowers me.

CONFERENCES

We live in a time where online presentations are available. We are able to get top-notch speakers who bring us research on learning. I often enjoy listening in while getting cozy in my comfortable chair or taking a hike on a walking trail. However, to me, they simply can't compete with an in-person conference. Although I have attended, and presented, at many conferences, I want to highlight my two favorites: the Festival of Education and ResearchED. These conferences are filled with evidence and research, and attended by teachers, leaders, and researchers. They are held on Saturdays and the price is incredibly affordable. All of the speakers donate their time to keep prices minimal. Both conferences feature prominent people in the research field. I find that I might be attending a presentation by a well-known researcher (and one of my edu-heroes) and then land up sitting by her in the next session. There is an air of camaraderie of like-minded people and you are guaranteed to leave with new friends and contacts. If ever these are in your area, *go*!

The inaugural United States **Festival of Education** was held in 2023 and sponsored by St. Andrew's Episcopal School and the CTTL (The Center for Transformative Teaching and Learning) (https://www.thecttl.org/) in Potomac, Maryland. This is a popular event in the UK and several of my UK edu-heroes were in attendance and presented.

ResearchED is my favorite conference. Tom Bennett OBE, of the UK, began this worldwide phenomenon. (For those of us not familiar with the initials: OBE stands for the Order of the British Empire, an extremely high honor. My favorite picture of Tom Bennett is when he was being awarded this honor by Prince William!) Tom felt there should be quality conferences, based on research and evidence, within an hour or two's distance, making them accessible to teachers, leaders, and researchers in the UK. The first in the United States was in 2019, in Philadelphia and organized by Eric Kalenz. I presented and I knew I had found a home in researchED. I have presented every year since, in wonderful cities and other countries including England and Canada. I have developed global friendships and each conference feels like a family reunion. The opportunities to network with people from your own town to those around the world, to widen your own evidence-based horizons, and to leave with research-informed material you will *use* makes this a conference all should attend. ResearchED conferences are now held all over the world (https://researched.org.uk/). A wealth of articles from researchED can be found at: https://researched.org.uk/articles/.

The science of learning exists and is expanding daily. You may be one of the lucky ones who work in a research-informed school. If not, this book is filled with contacts, links, and podcasts. Find your people! We're here.

Chapter **6**

Strategies

The time has come where we must redefine the strategies that lead to authentic learning. The following are strategies, based on evidence, I created for my students. If you are new to the science of learning, don't let these strategies overwhelm you. For everyone, start small. Pick a couple, try, and tweak. You do You!

MINI-QUIZ

The majority of my students had "mastered" the art of homework: Read a question, look up the answer, write it down, repeat. I felt it was my duty to grade the homework in the evening so it could be returned the following day. Due to the growth in my school district, it wasn't long before my 122 students per day had turned into over 180 students daily and the task of grading each night took approximately 2–2½ hours. My students generally scored quite well. However, I realized there was a total disconnect. If I were to ask the same questions to the class the following day, blank stares resulted. Deep discussions were nonexistent. When the research began in my classroom, my "aha moment" occurred when I realized my students were not retrieving at all. And the hours upon hours of teaching was not leading to learning. It was at that point I made a big change. The following year, I did not give homework. This may or may not work for you but it definitely worked for me. My task became: What could I substitute for homework that would lead to retrieval?

Mini-quiz.

I took what would have been homework, or discussions from class, and at the end of the day wrote them individually on slips of paper and put them in a small, red bucket. Here is how it worked:

1. At the beginning of class, I handed out small 2 inch × 3 inch pieces of recycled paper.

2. Students numbered 1–5 on the paper.

3. I randomly picked out five questions and read each to the class.

4. I collected the papers and went over the answers, providing immediate feedback.

5. I analyzed the mini-quizzes at the end of the day, adding feedback for each student.

6. The following day, the mini-quizzes were returned and we went over the answers again.

It was a very simple, but very effective, process. My two-plus hours of nightly grading turned into a 15-minute analysis after school. It was a low-stakes quiz. Students understood that this helped fine-tune their metacognition and helped them understand what they could retrieve and what needed more work.

```
Name:
1. _____
2. _____
3. _____
4. _____
5. _____
```

An example from my class.

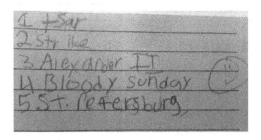

Here is a story I want to share. I had a mother attend a parent-teacher conference. She was a bit agitated and wanted to share a discussion she had with her son. She noted that he often did not do well on his mini-quizzes and asked him why. He replied, "Oh, Mom, if I don't do well on a mini-quiz, it just means my meta-cognition was telling me I wasn't able to retrieve it yet." She said to me, "What kind of answer is that?" I smiled and replied, "It is a great answer!" I discussed with the mother how her son learned and pulled up his grades. Every single test was 100%.

After years of giving traditional homework, changing to retrieval strategies boosted learning for my students. Although I traded mini-quizzes for traditional homework, high-stakes grades for tests, presentations, and projects were still given. And an added bonus was that by using the Power Tool strategies throughout the course of study, students were well prepared for the high stakes and review time was minimal.

Look at an example of another type of mini-quiz. It was given to 5th grade (~ age 10) science students by teacher Amber Haven.

Mini-quiz

1. What are the two "buzz" words when talking about forces?

   P _ _ _ _ _ ¢

   P _ _ _ _

2. Opposite poles on a magnet _ _ _ _ _ _ _, but same poles on a magnet _ _ _ _.

3. Gravity is a _ _ _ _ _ _ _ force, whereas buoyancy is a _ _ _ _ _ _ _ force.

4. When forces are balanced, does motion occur?

5. When forces act against each other, or in opposite directions, the forces applied are _ _ _ _ _ _ _.

BBQ

The BBQ strategy I used in my classroom stood for the "Big Basket Quiz." (Although I know science teachers who had BBQ stand for the Big Beaker Quiz.)

The procedure mirrors the mini-quiz; however, these were given once per week rather than daily.

Here is the procedure for mini-quizzes:

> I took what would have been homework, or discussions from class, and at the end of the day wrote them individually on slips of paper and put them in a small, red bucket. Here is how it worked:

1. At the beginning of class, I handed out small 2 inch × 3 inch pieces of recycled paper.

2. Students numbered 1–5 on the paper.

3. I randomly picked out five questions and read each to the class.

4. I collected the papers and went over the answers, providing immediate feedback.

5. I analyzed the mini-quizzes at the end of the day, adding feedback for each student.

6. The following day, the mini-quizzes were returned and we went over the answers again.

How BBQs differ: After I conducted my after-school analysis, I would look at all of the questions in the red bucket. Because I knew what was coming up in the curriculum and what students needed to retain, I took the questions that fell under those guidelines and put them in the Big Basket. Once per week, I would give the students a 10-question quiz using the questions from the basket. The questions could be from that particular week, a previous week, or a previous month or more.

Utilizing this strategy allowed students to use retrieval, spacing, interleaving, and metacognition.

FOUR STEPS OF METACOGNITION

I wanted to create a tool that would fit my vision for a science of learning criteria. It needed to

- allow students to retrieve,
- utilize spaced practice,
- give students opportunities to make judgments of learning,
- be low or no stakes,
- provide feedback,
- enable students to complete independently,
- act as a study tool, and
- reduce grading time for me.

The result was **The Four Steps of Metacognition.**

Four Steps of Metacognition

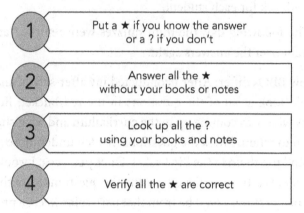

To make sense of how to use the Four Steps, let's first look at another strategy I created: *Retrieval Cards.*

RETRIEVAL CARDS

In my earlier years of teaching, I had students complete flash-cards: the drill of getting a list of terms, people, or places and having students write out the definitions from the back of the book. It was time-consuming for students to complete, for me to grade, and resulted in high effort and low impact. Students were merely copying information with no retrieval required. Unsurprisingly, these flashcards did not lead to deep discussions or knowledge retention. How could I create a tool that aligned with my science of learning criteria?

Let's look at an example of regular flashcards. Terms, people, and places were given and students looked up and recorded definitions.

Traditional Flashcards

TERM:	PERSON:

PLACE:	TERM:

Now let's take a look at how making the easy switch to retrieval cards enhances learning. Typically, I would create a sheet that included eight cards per page, although note cards could also be used. I often varied the cards; I might use terms and students complete the definition or, conversely, I might include the definition and students complete the term. I usually gave out the retrieval cards upon completion of a week-long lesson. The following section is an example where I include the person and you complete the definition.

Retrieval Card

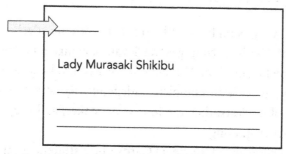

Lady Murasaki Shikibu

Your turn! Complete this Retrieval Card using the 4 Steps found on the following page.
(Verify according to Step 4, in Chapter 4!)

Following the Four Steps of Metacognition:

Step 1: At the arrow, on the line, students put a star if the answer is known or a question mark if it isn't. (Another option is using a happy face rather than a star.) This step is completed *without* using notes or writing down the answer. This allows for a student to make a judgment of learning. Typically, there would be several cards and the student would conduct this step for all of the cards at one time.

Step 2: Students retrieve the answers for all of their starred items – again, no notes or books. By challenging students to retrieve what they know without access to books or notes, students are better able to judge whether they truly know something or not.

Step 3: Now students focus on the items that they labeled with question marks: those items they were unsure of or didn't know. This is the first time students are able to use books and/or notes and use them to complete answers in the Retrieval Card.

Step 4: Students use their books/notes to verify that what they thought they knew was correct.

This very simple switch from traditional flashcards to Retrieval Cards encourages retrieval, spacing, and feedback-driven metacognition. The benefits of Retrieval Cards are that students are able to complete independently, students have a study tool for tests, they are low or no stakes, and they require little teacher-grading.

I looked over the Retrieval Cards upon student completion. Would the students submit Retrieval Cards with errors? Sometimes, yes, in the early phases of using this tool. If there was an error, I knew the student had not completed Step 4. I would not, however, point out where the error occurred, and the student would need to resubmit the cards. As students became invested in how these Retrieval Cards helped them study for exams (and reducing the time required for study), errors became minimal.

Now it's your turn to practice retrieval, spacing, and feedback-driven metacognition! Using the Four Steps to Metacognition, complete these Retrieval Cards. (And yes, write in your book!) Verify your answers by looking back at Chapter 4.

Your turn! Try it!	
_____ _____ This boosts learning by mixing up closely related topics, encouraging discrimination between similarities and differences.	Spacing _____ _____
_____ Retrieval _____ _____	_____ This boosts learning by providing the opportunity for students to discriminate what they know from what they don't.

Step 1: Make a Judgment of Learning. Star if you know it, question mark if you don't.

Step 2: Answer all you know.

Step 3: Look up those you don't know.

Step 4: Verify your correct answers.

Retrieval Cards Template

Create a table and insert lines!

Metacognition Sheet

I usually had students complete Retrieval Cards after each lesson
or chapter. I wanted to take all of the Power Tools a step farther
and create a strategy that students would complete closer to an
exam. Again, I looked at my science of learning criteria and the

result became the Metacognition Sheet. Here is an example from my classroom:

☆	?	Items to Know	Answer
		Maximilien Robespierre	
		Definition of "revolution"	
		How did the lives of working people change as a result of revolutions?	
		How did revolutions change social pyramids of power?	

Similar to Retrieval Cards, the Four Steps of Metacognition are used.

How are these two strategies similar and different?

1. Retrieval Cards contain content from, usually, a week-long lesson, whereas Metacognition Sheets include content from an entire chapter or unit (often 4–6 lessons). Metacognition Sheets could be one page or longer.

2. Retrieval Cards ask students to retrieve key terms and definitions, whereas Metacognition Sheets ask students to answer not only key terms and definitions but also essential questions and complex ideas. My students also knew that just because particular questions were on the Metacognition Sheet, it did not necessarily mean these questions would be on a test. They knew questions may be asked for spacing, for students to retrieve information that may need to be used in later chapters.

Here is your turn to work on a Metacognition Sheet:			

☆	?	Items to Know	Answer
		Who was the Japanese princess who lived around 1000 CE who is often credited for writing the world's first novel?	
		Patrice Bain has 8 science of learning criteria for developing strategies. Name 4.	
		Why are Retrieval Cards more beneficial than traditional Flashcards?	

Metacognition Sheet Template

☆	?	Items to Know	Answer

Here is an example of another type of Metacognition Sheet; credit to 5th-grade teacher: Amber Haven. Rather than using the Four Steps, students use JOL (Judgments of Learning) to guide their test preparation.

Test Date (put the date of the **test**, rather than current date, ensuring students have a visual reminder).

Unit 1: Scientists at Work Metacognition Sheet

Please read through the Metacognition Sheet. Put an "X" in the column that you feel describes your feelings about each concept. Study by asking yourself questions and referring to your notes until you can put an "X" next to all of the concepts in the "Got It!" section.

Concepts to know:	Got It!	Need to Study It
I can identify the difference between testable and nontestable questions. Examples: (testable/nontestable) Which color of rose attracts the most bees? (testable/nontestable) Does running in place for 30 seconds increase heart rate? (testable/nontestable) Which color of rose smells the best? (testable/nontestable) Are 5th-grade girls or 5th-grade boys taller?		
The independent variable is what I'm testing in an experiment.		
There is only _____ independent variable in the experiment. It is the thing that can be _____ (e.g.: Coke vs. Diet Coke, changing the height of the ramp for the toy cars, the number of Alka-Seltzers put into the canister).		

(continued)

Concepts to know:	Got It!	Need to Study It
The _____ variable is the data I collect during an experiment (e.g.: the amount of Coke or Diet Coke left in the bottle, the distance the toy car travels, the distance the cap shoots off of the canister).		
The _____ variable is measured and can be placed into a data table.		
The _____ variables must stay the same throughout an experiment.		
I can usually identify at least _____ control variables in an experiment.		
Tools for measuring: _____ tape, graduated _____, balance _____, beaker, spring _____.		
Tools for observing: _____lens, _____scope, magnifying _____.		
Measuring tape: measure _____ in _____ (_____).		
Graduated cylinder: measure _____ in _____ (_____).		
Balance scale: measure _____ in _____ (_____).		
Beaker: measure _____ in _____ (_____).		
Spring scale: measure _____ in _____ (_____).		
The order of the scientific method is: _____, _____, _____, _____ (record data), make a _____, _____ (analyze data).		

Concepts to know:	Got It!	Need to Study It
A _____ is an educated guess.		
A scientist cannot perform an experiment only once. He/She should conduct the experiment at least ___ times (3 _____, or over a length of time).		
The volume of an object can be found by seeing the rise of liquid in a graduated cylinder. See diagram, for example: The volume of the chalk is _____ milliliters (ml) because the liquid started out at _____ ml, and after adding the chalk, it rose to _____ ml. The liquid raised _____ ml after adding the chalk, so that is the volume of the piece of chalk.		

Scientists use models for _____ reasons.		
Reason 1: Models are used to represent things ___ _____ to see without powerful technology.		
Reason 2: Models are used to_____ _____ things too large to see as a whole, or hold and manipulate for studying purposes.		
Reason 3: Models are used to represent things ____ _____ _____ or available.		
Reason 4: Models are used to _____ things that have not yet happened.		
Reason 5: Models can be used to represent things that may be hard to get to or manipulate because they are hidden _____ or _____ other things.		

RETRIEVAL GUIDES

I was one of those students who took copious notes. I wrote from the beginning of class until the bell rang. I rarely looked up and feared the amount of information I missed. Worst of all, my notes were a jumbled mess and were of little use when test preparation began. I vowed I would not do that to my students. But what was the alternative? Looking at my criteria, I created Retrieval Guides.

My 11-year-old students were often novices to World History because it was the first time in my district's curriculum that it was taught. In addition, the terms were often very difficult to pronounce (Queen Amanashaketo, being one of my favorites). I didn't want my students stumbling over new words and ideas so we read our text aloud in class and I had created "study guides" or outlines for each lesson. Students had these in front of them and could go back, find the answers in the text, and copy them down. I soon realized, however, that this was similar to flashcards. Students were simply copying down information. The research in my classroom led me to know that retrieval was required.

I turned my "study guides" into "Retrieval Guides" with ease and I turned copying into retrieval. I knew precisely the information I wanted my students to record. When we got to that point in the guide, I would simply say, "Let's retrieve" and I would pause. Books would close or, if during a lecture or presentation, a blank screen would be shown, and students would *pull out* the information rather than copy. I might do a "Turn and Talk" and discussion, and then back to the reading, lecture, or presentation. This required minimal time and reaped huge rewards – including having perfectly organized notes at the end of class! Another big win was how the students retained the information better and we were able to have rich discussions.

This strategy works well with most ages. (For younger students, I encourage using more of a "close" where most of the information is already there and they simply write a word or draw a picture.) I also consistently use Retrieval Guides when giving professional development. A procedure for my class and professional development presentations: When someone is talking, all writing utensils and devices are down.

Here is an example from my classroom:

Chapter 13 Lesson 2: Empires of East Africa

Introduction: By the 700s, empires rich in gold – Ghana, Mali, Songhai – began to emerge in western Africa.

I. **Ghana: An Early Empire**

    A. Ghana's capital city: _____

    B. Describe the king's court in Ghana's capital city (or draw on back of paper):

        _____
        _____
        _____
        _____

    C. Merchants allowed to handle only _____
        _____

    D. Supply and Demand: items that are _____ are high in value because they are not easy to get.

For older students, my Retrieval Guides would be in outline form but the categories would be left blank. I would give the category at the time I paused for retrieval. An advantage for using blank outlines for older students is they can't work ahead. As the teacher, I knew precisely what information I wanted my students to retrieve and knew exactly when to pause. At the end of class, each student has the information needed, in an organized fashion, and will make study for test preparation easier.

For example:

I. **Ghana: An Early Empire**

    A. _____

    B. _____:

        _____
        _____
        _____
        _____

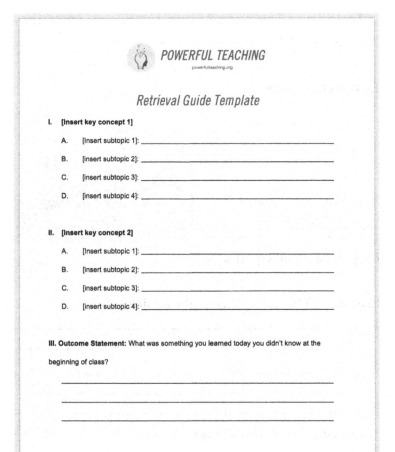

POWERFUL TEACHING
powerfulteaching.org

Retrieval Guide Template

I. **[Insert key concept 1]**

    A.   [Insert subtopic 1]: _____

    B.   [Insert subtopic 2]: _____

    C.   [Insert subtopic 3]: _____

    D.   [Insert subtopic 4]: _____

II. **[Insert key concept 2]**

    A.   [Insert subtopic 1]: _____

    B.   [Insert subtopic 2]: _____

    C.   [Insert subtopic 3]: _____

    D.   [Insert subtopic 4]: _____

III. Outcome Statement: What was something you learned today you didn't know at the beginning of class?

_____

_____

_____

1

This template can be found at www.powerfulteaching .org/resources

No note-taking (which always brings forth gasps!) but continue with explaining Retrieval Guides. I practice what I preach and want teachers to see firsthand how to make the simple switch from copying notes to implementing retrieval.

Look at the example of a Retrieval Guide I use with teachers when giving a presentation on *Powerful Teaching*.[1]

Retrieval Guide

Pooja K. Agarwal & Patrice M. Bain

Session 1: Unleash the Science of Learning

1. _____
   _____ ⟶ _____

2. _____ : _____
   _____
   _____

3. <u>Spacing: Retrieval/teaching over time</u>

   <u>Interleaving: Comparing and contrasting similar content</u>
   <u>Metacognition: Differentiating the known from the unknown</u>

   _____
   _____
   _____
   _____
   _____
   _____

4. _____ : _____

_____

_____

_____

_____

5. Questions to Ponder/Concepts to Deep Dive: _____

_____

_____

_____

_____

www.patricebain.com

patrice@patricebain.com

www.powerfulteaching.org

X (formerly Twitter): @patricebain1

RETRIEVE-TAKING

Retrieve-taking is similar to Retrieval Guides and it is a method for students to take notes; the main difference is that Retrieve-taking often doesn't use a formal outline.

How to turn note-taking into Retrieve-taking:

- Pencils/devices down while teacher presents lesson (lecture, video, presentation . . . works for all methods).

- As soon as vital information is taught/discussed, pause the lesson.

- Students write notes.**

- Teacher gives feedback/verifies information.
- Continue lesson, again no pencils or devices.

  ** i.e. Notes could be taken as:

- Two Things: write down two things that you think played a pivotal role.
- Brain Dump: In 30 seconds, retrieve what you think was important.
- Having a "Retrieve-taking Notebook" allows students to keep all notes in one place.

This is such a simple strategy to implement. It is important to give students a brief, limited time to take notes, verify information, and continue on. One of the obstacles I had to overcome was the students' mindsets of hurriedly taking notes while I spoke. By consistently reinforcing the "no writing utensils while someone is speaking" procedure, students gained confidence that time would be given to take notes. A benefit of this strategy is that students began listening differently in class, discussions became richer, and students had well-organized notes at the end of class that provided rich study material.

Power Tools used: Because the teacher plans what is taught and when to pause, it is likely all four Power Tools are used.

I created and used a form for teachers and leaders when presenting professional development. The same procedures are used.

Name: _____   School: _____

Biggest Takeaways:	Strategies to Implement:
Questions to Ponder:	Concept to Deep Dive

Start	Stop	Keep

powerfulteaching.org   @patricebain1   patrice@patricebain.com   retrievalpatrice.org

Let's try Retrieve-taking!

1. What are two things you have learned about strategies?

   A. _____

   _____

   B. _____

   _____

2. What is a strategy you would like to try? _____

_____

Why?

_____

_____

_____

_____

POWER TICKET

I created the Power Ticket because I wanted a strategy that incorporated all of the Power Tools and gave students the opportunity to see connections, conduct deep dives into Essential Questions, and have the ability to compare and contrast facts and ideas.

Power Ticket: What did we learn. . .?

	Today?	Yester-day?	Last Week?	Last Month?	Last Quarter?	Last Semester?
Topic						
Fact 1						
Fact 2						
Fact 3						

As the teacher, you understand the critical learning required for your curriculum. You can use this strategy to direct and lead the students by the topics you choose. I chose to incorporate a theme through an Essential Question and drove the discussion to include deep thinking.

Power Tickets can be completed during one class period. However, I often stretched mine out as a retrieval exercise using approximately five minutes (or less) of class each day for a week. For example, I might spend five minutes on the categories of Today, Yesterday, and Last Week. My method was usually for students to complete Fact 1. They would need to get Fact 2 from a peer. We would have a group discussion and the student would complete Fact 3 from information gathered at our discussion. On the following days, I would spend about the same amount of time on each of the remaining topics. The final project was often an essay answering the Essential Question citing examples through history.

There are reasons I use this strategy: It helps students to organize big ideas and facts into deep and critical thinking for essay writing and minimizes opportunities for plagiarism. Students submit this form along with their essays.

Here is an example from my class:

Power Ticket: How does conflict impact society? (Essential Question)

	Today?	Yester-day?	Last Week?	Last Month?	Last Quarter?	Last Semester?
Topic	Vietnam War	Cold War Alliances	China's Cultural Revolution	WWII	French Revolution	Ancient Rome
Fact 1						
Fact 2						
Fact 3						

RETRIEVAL DICE

This is an activity which may incorporate all of the Power Tools. Simply choose the items you would like to have students retrieve, insert them in the boxes, and let the students cut out, fold on the lines, and glue the tabs. An option is to have several different dice available. Students can use it independently or with groups. If used as a type of review, I would include a Metacognition Sheet enabling students to target what information needs further study.

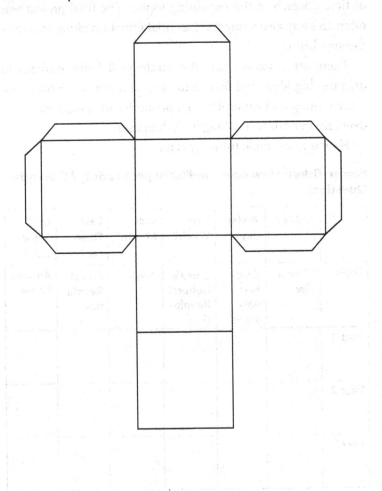

Photocopy, cut out, glue flaps, and retrieve!

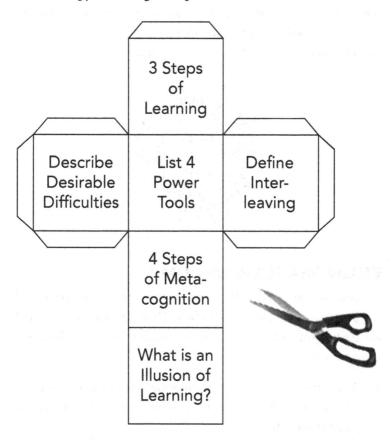

I did not create the following strategies yet I used them for so many years they are a part of my pedagogical toolbox. Unfortunately, I am unable to give credit where credit is due.

BLAST FROM THE PAST

This is one of my favorite strategies and I used it multiple times daily! It requires no material and can be done in less than 30 seconds. What is required? Thinking ahead to your big-ticket items that require spaced practice. A simple, "It's Time for a Blast from the Past!" shoutout followed by a question, about 5 seconds for students to think, a Turn and Talk and a group share. Retrieval, spacing, and metacognition – and no grading!

BRAIN DRAIN/BRAIN DUMP

Brain Drains are an effective strategy that can be used in several ways and most require no grading. However, feedback should always be given and can be done through Turn and Talks and a group share.

- After discussing important information in class, reading a text, or in the midst of a presentation, have students write a quick summary.
- Use a Brain Drain as an entrance or exit ticket.
- Use *in lieu* of a chapter test.
- Use as an addition to a chapter test: What else do you know about _____ that wasn't on the test?

Usually, my tests included multiple choice questions and essays. However, one of my favorites was using a Brain Drain. At the conclusion of studying ancient Egypt, students were prepared for the usual multiple-choice questions and essay. However, as they sat down, ready for the test, I simply gave them a piece of paper that stated:

What do you know about ancient Egypt?

And the students wrote and wrote and wrote. *All* of my students, regardless of their ability level, wrote. Comments I frequently heard were: "I would think of one thing and that would spark something else and then THAT would spark something else!" or, "Oh, the bell! I could have written so much more!" It was not unusual to receive five (or more!) pages written front and back. A requirement was that each correct statement must reflect something we had learned in class.

The downside was that because it was the chapter test, I graded them. (And, yes, it took a weekend to grade the 180+ tests!) My chapter tests were usually worth 100 points; for a Brain Drain, 70+ correct statements earned an A, 60–69 for a B, etc. Accommodations in the grading scale were made if it was required in a student's Individualized Education Plan (IEP).

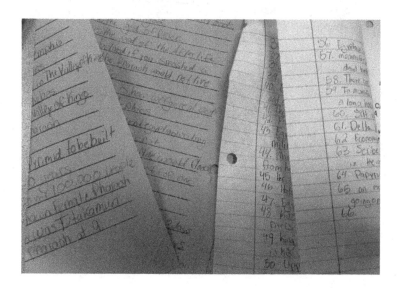

Every year, I showed these to parents at parent–teacher conferences. Without fail, when showing them to parents whose children were in special education classes, I would see tears. It was the first time for many parents that they were to go beyond seeing multiple-choice questions or more simple versions of tests; this was authentic learning, and I often heard many positive comments from them. For many, it was as if they could *see* right into their children's minds for the first time.

Look at the infographics I adapted based on Dr. Pooja Agarwal's guide, *How to Implement Retrieval-based Learning in Early Childhood Education.*

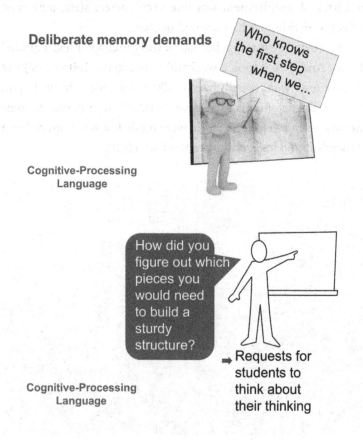

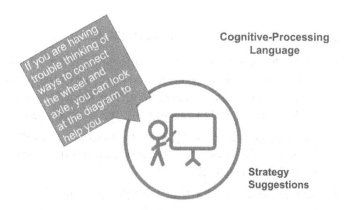

Cognitive-Processing Language

Strategy Suggestions

ANTONIA PANTOJA PREPARATORY ACADEMY

I would like to thank Michael-Joseph Mercanti-Anthony, Ed.D., for sharing the following resource. Dr. Mercanti-Anthony is principal of the Antonia Pantoja Preparatory Academy, a member of the Greenwich, Connecticut, School Board, and the Chair of the 2024 researchED conference held in Greenwich. This "Common Instructional Strategies" tool is a living document that can be changed and added to; it provides a common language and strategies for schools to follow.

Antonia Pantoja Preparatory Academy

Common Instructional Strategies

"Building the APPA Way!"

At Antonia Pantoja Preparatory Academy (APPA), we use Dr. Karen Hess's Cognitive Rigor Matrix[2] to consistently challenge students at high levels of cognitive complexity. The common strategies below support student learning across the depth of knowledge (DOK) spectrum, so that they can meet the demands of daily learning at DOK levels 3 and 4.

(continued)

Strategy #1: The "Brain Dump" (DOK 1)

1. Make the question specific to a recent topic (i.e. "Write down everything you can remember" about the parts of a cell, the process of skimming, the impact of industrialization, multiple ways to solve this problem, etc.).

2. Strategy can be employed in the beginning, middle, or end of the lesson (i.e. success starter, during mini-lesson, or exit ticket).

3. Include sentence stems that set the criteria.

4. During the exercise, encourage engagement by prompting specific students who need it.

5. Promote success through participation and effort: *Not graded for accuracy.*

Strategy #2: "Power Ticket" (DOK 1)

1. Students independently complete a chart challenging them to bring to mind concepts from previous lessons.

2. The chart can challenge students to retrieve information from over the length of the unit or go back to information earlier in the year.

3. The chart can be modified based on student needs, including sentence stems, word bank, or vocabulary. These "hints" could be up front, or given to students after a few minutes of independent retrieval.

4. Once completed, students collaborate to add to their chart with a partner.

5. Promote success through participation and effort: *Not graded for accuracy.*

What did we talk about...

semester?	Today?	Yesterday?	Last week?	Last month?	Last quarter?	Last
	[insert Concept 1]	[insert Concept 2]	[insert Concept 3]	[insert Concept 4]	[insert Concept 5]	[insert Concept 6]
Write one fact						
Write a second fact						
Write a third fact						

Strategy #3: Specialized Instruction in Integrated Co-Teaching (ICT) (DOK 2–3)

Avoid One-Teach/One-Assist, but instead consider, "How can this lesson be different to take advantage of multiple teachers being in the room?"

Alternative Teaching:

- While the general education teacher facilitates a larger group, specialist teachers work with a small group to reteach a concept or develop skills.

- Also known as "Reteach and Enrichment."

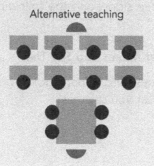

Alternative teaching

(continued)

Station Teaching for Specialized Instruction

- Students grouped homogeneously based on need.
- Students cycle through different stations, one facilitated by the general education teacher, at least one by a specialist teacher, and one of independent work.
- Stations are timed and the process may extend over multiple days.
- All students cycle through the stations, but stations may change based on the needs of that group. For example, a special education teacher may reteach a concept with one group, but provide enrichment to another group as they cycle through his/her station.

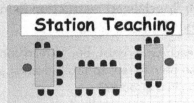

Strategy #4: Metacognitive Routines (DOK 3–4)

Metacognition is when students think about their thinking. By planning for, monitoring, and evaluating their learning, students strengthen their understanding. Red, yellow, and green signs[3] and the following routines support this work.

Routine 1: What Makes You Say That

- Essential Questions: What's going on? What do you see that makes you say that?

- Purpose: Cultivates observation, description, explanation-building, and evidence-based reasoning. Because students share their interpretations, they are encouraged to see multiple perspectives.

- Application: Use this routine when you want students to look closely at something and uncover their reasoning.

- For link to template see footnote.[4]

Routine 2: See, Think, Wonder

- Essential Questions: What do you see? What do you think about that? What does it make you wonder?

  - Purpose: Encourages students to think carefully about why something looks the way it does or is the way it is.

  - Application: Use this routine with a relevant object (such as an artwork, image, artifact, chart, video, etc.).

(continued)

- Launch: At the beginning of a new unit to motivate student interest; during the unit of study to create connections; near the end of a unit to encourage students to further apply their knowledge and ideas.

- For link to template see footnote.[5]

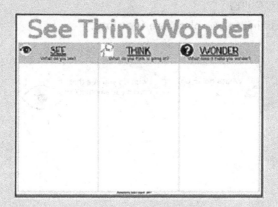

Routine 3: I Used to Think, Now I Think. . .

- Purpose: Students reflect on their thinking about a topic or issue and explore how and why their thinking has changed.

- Application: Used to consolidate learning when students' initial thinking is likely to have changed as a result of a learning experience.

- Possible approach:
  - "When we began our study of _____, you had some initial ideas about it. Take a minute to remember what ideas you previously had about _____. Write a few sentences using the sentence starter, 'I used to think. . .'"

- For link to template see footnote.[6]

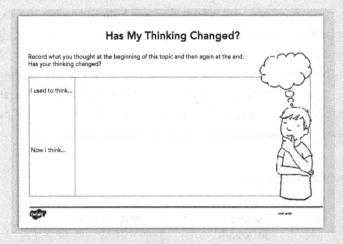

Common Classroom Features

1. **Success Starter:** Classes should traditionally begin with an independent warm-up activity posted for students to complete (i.e. Brain Dump or other question).

2. **Learning Target:** The day's objective should be posted in a permanent place for students to reference throughout the period. Most days, the learning target should be at DOK 3 or 4.

3. **Closure:** Lessons should end with a closing activity (such as an exit ticket or Brain Dump) that allows students to consolidate their understanding of the day's learning target.

STRATEGIES FROM OTHERS

The following people have graciously granted permission to use their strategies. Many of these can be downloaded for free. I will begin with Kate Jones from the UK. Kate began her career as a teacher and graces us with her strategies, books, podcasts, and webinars.

Kate Jones's Strategies

Kate Jones is a gift to educators. She has written several books on learning, memory, and retrieval. I was honored to be in two of her books, writing about working with parents and the "teaching triangle" and, secondly, talking about my Big Basket Quizzes. She can be found on podcasts and webinars. She graciously shares her strategies and has united teachers globally. These strategies are hers and there are many more available in her Retrieval Series of books.

Revision Bookmark

Download the Revision Bookmark for free:
https://www.tes.com/teaching-resource/revision-bookmark-12204148

Retrieval Practice Placemat

The Retrieval Practice Placemat is a great tool and infographic for students. It promotes retrieval, spacing, and metacognition. It could easily be used for entrance and exit activities.

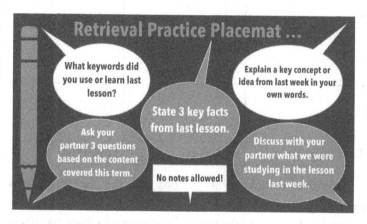

The Retrieval Practice Placemat be downloaded for free at:
https://www.tes.com/teaching-resource/retrieval-practice-placemat-12270272

Think and Link (Kate Jones)

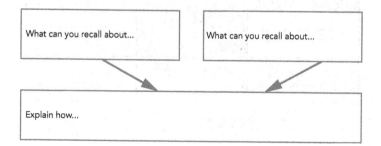

Think and Link is a great strategy for implementing interleaving and promoting deep thinking – and you know it works! You've done it!

Retrieval Challenge Grid (Kate Jones)

How many points can you get?		
Last Lesson	Last Week	Last Term

Kate Jones assigns points per box with the "last term" worth more.

Retrieval, spacing, interleaving, and metacognition. It's all here!

Retrieval Practice Challenge Grid (Kate Jones)

Retrieval Practice Challenge Grid

Insert question from further back	Insert question based on content from last week	Insert question based on content from two weeks ago
Insert question based on content from two weeks ago	Insert question from further back	Insert question based on content from last week
Insert question based on content from last lesson	Insert question based on content from two weeks ago	Insert question from further back
Insert question from further back	Insert question based on content from last week	Insert question based on content from last lesson

One Point – Last lesson	Two Points – Last week	Three Points – Two weeks ago	Four Points – Further back

Download the template for free:
https://www.tes.com/en-us/teaching-resource/retrieval-practice-challenge-grid-blank-template-12270273

The Learning Grid (Kate Jones)

The Learning Grid.
Roll the dice and describe the keyword. Roll again and put the two words into a sentence.

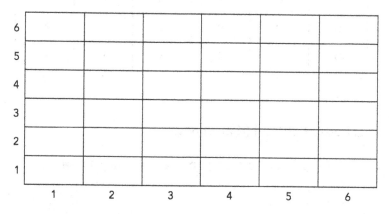

One of the ways this strategy can be used is by the teacher filling in the boxes with vocabulary terms. An alternative would be to have definitions in the boxes. When a dice is rolled, each student writes the term in the same box, next to the definition. This strategy also works well with foreign languages. Because the teacher has control of completing the boxes, retrieval, spacing, interleaving, and feedback-driven metacognition can be used.

The Literacy Grid.

Roll the dice and name a keyword starting with that letter. Roll again and put the two words into a sentence.

6	A	D	I	E	R	T
5	B	R	B	L	E	M
4	D	L	O	M	L	N
3	A	D	I	E	R	T
2	B	R	R	L	B	M
1	D	L	O	N	L	N
	1	2	3	4	5	6

Vocabulary Retrieval (Kate Jones)

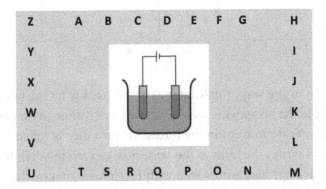

Z	A	B	C	D	E	F	G	H
Y								I
X								J
W								K
V								L
U	T	S	R	Q	P	O	N	M

Letters can be used as a prompt and the image in the middle as a cue.

Learners write as many keywords associated with that image by the letters.

Incorporating Power Tools through a Teacher's Perspective

The following are activities and strategies from teacher Amber Haven. She has embraced evidence-informed strategies and I would like to highlight how she uses them in the framework of a 5th-grade curriculum. In her science class, she uses the Fifth-grade Next Generation Science Standards (NGSS). In addition to the content standards, Mrs. Haven interleaves scientific skills throughout her activities. She takes her students outside daily and asks them to think like scientists. They choose aspects of nature, use photography, and make daily records of their findings. Each student has a measuring tape, their scientific log, and access to a camera. They collaborate, make predictions, observations, and analyze data. They are using retrieval, spacing, metacognition, and interleaving.

The following two examples use interleaving through the use of Essential Questions.

Example 1. The following standard is used: Fifth-grade NGSS 5-ESS1-2 Earth's Place in the Universe | Next Generation Science Standards[7] states:

> Students who demonstrate understanding can: represent data in graphical displays to reveal patterns of daily changes in length and direction of shadows. . .

The students took daily observations and measurements of a particular tree were guided by the Essential Question: How and why do shadows change?

September 26th, 2023 10:45 a.m. Length of Shadow: 986 cm	November 16th, 2023 10:39 a.m. Length of Shadow: 1,532 cm	February 13th, 2024 10:45 a.m. Length of Shadow: 1,396 cm	March 18th, 2024 10:45 a.m. Length of Shadow: 1,158 cm

Difference in shadow lengths: 1,532 cm – 986 cm = 546 cm	Difference in shadow lengths: 1,532 cm – 1,396 cm = 136 cm	Difference in shadow lengths: 1,396 cm – 1,158 cm = 238 cm

Example 2. The following were the Essential Questions used:

1. How do the sunrises and sunsets show that the Earth is in a different position around the sun?

2. How does air pressure impact the weather we experience?

3. What is the difference between weather and climate?

4. Using the cross-cutting concept, analyze measurements and observations through models.

Here are data students were compiling:

3/11–3/14	Real Temp °F/C	Feel Like Temp °F/C	Humidity %	Air Pressure inHg	Moon Phase	Sunrise a.m Sunset p.m	Out the Door
Monday	41F/5C 50F/10C 58F/14C	37F/3C 48F/9C 55F/13C	68% 52% 39%	30.23inHg 30.22inHg 30.20inHg	Waxing crescent Rise: 8:04 a.m. Set: 8:57 p.m.	Rise: 7:17 a.m. Set: 8.57 p.m.	Long-term observation
Tuesday	F53/12C F58/14C 65F/18C	F51/11C F57/14C 65F/18C	59% 50% 43%	30.02inHg 30.01inHg 29.98inHg	Waxing crescent Rise: a.m. Set: p.m.	Rise: 7:15 a.m. Set: 7:05 p.m.	Long-term measurement
Wednesday	F58/C F62/17C F68/20C	F57/C F61/16C F69/21C	72% 66% 58%	29.84inHg 29.84inHg 29.83inHg	Waxing crescent Rise: 8:04 a.m. Set: 8:57 p.m.	Rise: 7:13 a.m. Set: 7:06 p.m.	Current Unit: observation
Thursday	F/C F/C F/C	F/C F/C F/C	% % %	inHg inHg inHg	Waxing crescent Rise: 9:03 a.m. Set: 11:28 p.m.	Rise: 8:04 a.m. Set: 8:57 p.m.	Current Unit: measurement
Friday	F/C F/C F/C	F/C F/C F/C	94% % %	inHg inHg inHg	Waxing crescent Rise: 8:04 p.m. Set: 8:57 a.m.	Rise: a.m. Set: p.m.	Free Investigation Friday

These examples expand beyond what students learn from a textbook and illustrate how retrieval, spacing, interleaving, and metacognition can be incorporated into curriculum.

Parent Communication

In the United States, many schools have adopted the Danielson Framework[8] for evaluations. We know that school–home communication is important (and is found in the framework:

Domain 4, c: Engaging Families and Communities). Teachers sending home a weekly newsletter is common. Mrs. Haven took this a step farther and created an opportunity not only to meet this framework, but also to use it as a tool to:

- keep parents informed.

- utilize as an opportunity for retrieval, spacing, and metacognition.

- improve students' technical skills.

- improve writing skills.

As Mrs. Haven states: "Students are expected to communicate with their guardians each week. This communication allows students to take ownership of their grades, their academic progress, and their social/emotional growth. These weekly assignments can be taken as a grade."

During the first semester, students write notes, letters, postcards, etc., to their families. For the second semester, students write emails to their adults at home.

Parents told Mrs. Haven, "I used to ask 'How was your day?' and I usually received a one-word answer. Now, we actually have dialogues and conversations!" In addition, parents, and carers have guided information that provides opportunities for retrieval, spacing, and metacognition. (And what parent wouldn't love to have this type of insight into their ten-year-old child's school day?) Look at the example of a guideline students use. Mrs. Haven has also generously shared her template.[9]

Email Formatting Reminders:	Email Content Requirements:
Greeting: Capital D, Capital Family Member's Name, comma afterwards, then press "Enter" TWICE	Dear Guardian,
Paragraph 1: Quick introduction. Then press "Enter" TWICE	-Write 5 paragraphs, each with a minimum of 5 sentences. Add specific details! -Use proper capitalization and punctuation throughout the entire email
Paragraph 2: Grades and PBIS Report. Type 5 or more complete sentences. Then press "Enter" TWICE	-Discuss your grades -Discuss your PBIS account
Paragraph 3: Academic Report. Discuss your classes in complete sentences. You can give lots of detail about one class, or you can give little detail about lots of classes. Then press "Enter" TWICE	-Tell something fun, something challenging, and something boring about your classes this week
Paragraph 4: Social Report. Write 5 or more complete sentences about your friends, about what is happening outside of school, and/or anything on your mind. Then Press "Enter" TWICE	-Explain anything going on in your friend group, your goals for finishing your 5th-grade year, your events going on outside of school (sports, dance, music, etc.), or just tell your adults anything else that's on your mind
Paragraph 5: Important Dates. List these dates. The list can be in complete sentences, or you can use bullet points. Then press "Enter" TWICE	-Explain upcoming dates
Paragraph 6: Technology Challenge. Press "Enter" TWICE. Then type your name.	-Take a picture of yourself with your laptop and add it to the email OR find a video or a link to send to your family
Closing: Capital Sincerely followed by a comma. Press "Enter" ONCE. Then type your name.	Sincerely, Your Name

Six Strategies Infographic

It is always a joy to discover how *Powerful Teaching* has had an impact. This infographic was created by Dr. Wes Hobbs, who at the time was at Middle Tennessee State University in Murfreesboro, Tennessee. He is now the Assistant Principal at Delk-Henson Intermediate School in Chapel Hill, Tennessee. He can be followed on X (formerly Twitter): @crashthebored

6 Strategies

Inspired by the work of AGARWAL & BAIN

FOR POWERFUL TEACHING

To help with Retrieval, Spacing, and Interleaving

BRAIN DUMP

– After allowing time (4+ days) for students to forget material, give students a time limit (2 to 5 minutes) to write as much about a topic as they can remember. Research shows the struggle to recall, adds to the ability to remember the next time.

2 THINGS

– After allowing time (2+ days) for students to forget material, have students write "2 Things" they remember about a topic. Have them share their facts with a partner, then in a group of four. This spaced, retrieval practice, while also using group think, will be helpful in having information stick.

TL; DR

– Too Long – Didn't Read! Challenge your students to summarize articles/novels read many days ago, using only 240 characters (Tweet), or using only six words (6 Word Summary).

FLIP IT AND REVERSE IT

– Instead of giving homework on the lesson you went over today, give homework on the lesson you went over last week. The struggle to recall, partnered with interleaving it with current material is pure gold!

THE WEEKLY MIXUP

– Provide students a "daily or weekly mix-up" of all things covered up to that point in the year. This hits all types of practice: retrieval, spaced, and interleaved. Can be short... 5 to 10 Questions.

4 STEPS OF METACOGNITION

– Teach students to use the 4 Steps of Metacognition when answering their "Weekly Mix-Ups"
  1. Put a STAR ✭ beside the question if you know it, and a "?" if you don't know it.
  2. Answer all stars.
  3. Look ?'s up using notes/books.
  4. Verify all stars are correct by using notes/books.

Brain Pops

Here is an infographic created and posted from Ana Henderson and the Teaching and Learning Group of Loughborough Grammar School in Loughborough, England. It is a joy to see *Powerful Teaching* influencing strategies around the globe!

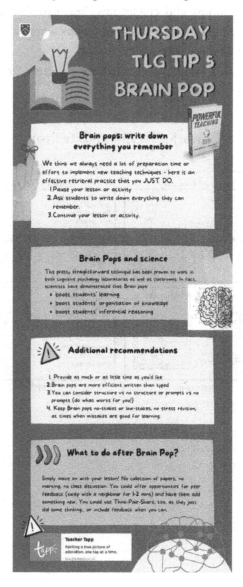

Zeph Bennett's Infographics

The following infographics are from England's Zeph Bennett. He generously shares his work; I have used many of his infographics for years in my presentations. These work very well in professional development. Copy them as posters and post them in teacher workrooms and classrooms. You can find Zeph on X (formerly Twitter): @Pegeekscorner. Zeph's work can be found at Bitesize CPD & Presentations.[10]

The first two infographics illustrate concepts from *Powerful Teaching*.[11]

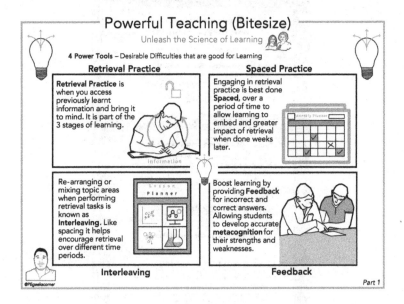

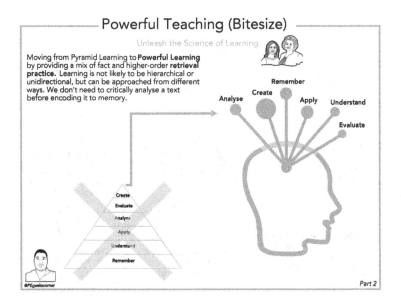

The next two infographics give options for retrieval. Another option would be to give students a topic and let them choose the method of retrieval.

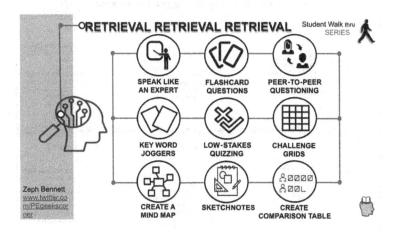

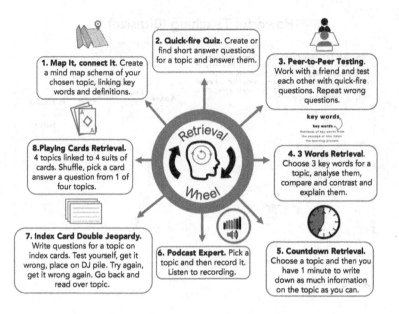

The next infographic illustrates how we learn.

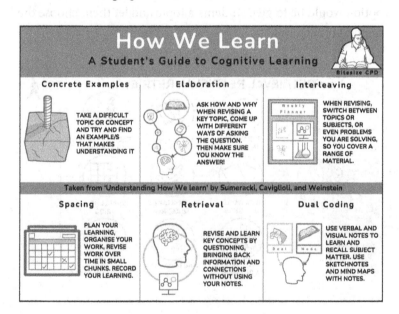

Look at the infographic on how we remember.

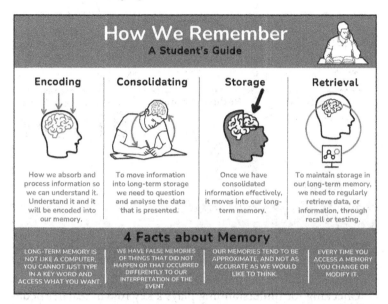

Review the infographics illustrating good practice for teachers and students when devising presentations.

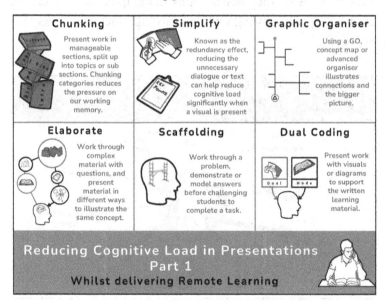

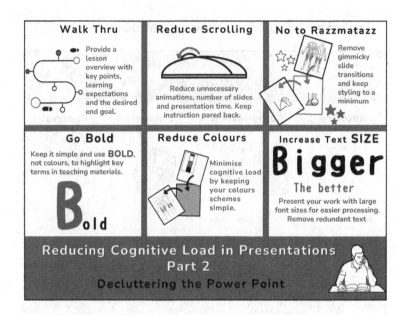

Checking for understanding plays a key role in teacher pedagogy. It helps the teacher ensure students are getting the information and the feedback helps students discriminate what they know from what they don't. Zeph's infographic states it can be used as "Options during Online Learning" and also works well in person.

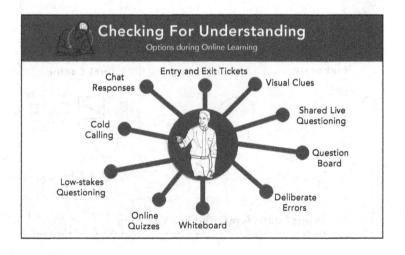

I want to conclude this chapter with a powerful infographic. I was honored to be asked to be a contributor to the UNESCO (United Nations Education, Science, and Cultural Organization) ISEE assessment.

"**The International Science and Evidence Based Education (ISEE) Assessment**[12] is an initiative of the UNESCO Mahatma Gandhi Institute of Education for Peace and Sustainable Development (MGIEP), and is its contribution to the Futures of Education process launched by UNESCO Paris in September 2019. In order to contribute to re-envisioning the future of education with a science and evidence-based report, UNESCO MGIEP embarked on the first-ever large-scale assessment of knowledge of education." It outlines the goals and vision for worldwide education by the year 2030.

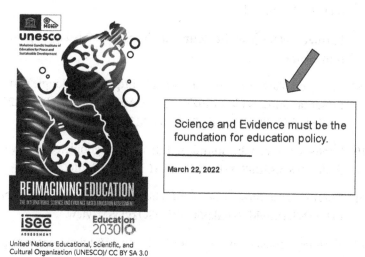

Science and Evidence must be the foundation for education policy.

March 22, 2022

United Nations Educational, Scientific, and Cultural Organization (UNESCO)/ CC BY SA 3.0

NOTES

1. Agarwal, Pooja K., and Patrice M. Bain. *Powerful Teaching: Unleash the Science of Learning.* San Francisco: Jossey-Bass, 2019.

2. More details on Dr. Karen Hess's Cognitive Rigor Matrix can be found at https://www.karin-hess.com/cognitive-rigor-and-dok.

3. More details on this student assessment tool can be found at https://docs.google.com/document/d/1IdsWSnnNmCaZdSJA 5Qnp0Q-BTUfQJbVY6zpLJ5-4cCU/edit.

4. The template can be found at https://drive.google.com/file/d/ 1M1odZxAV8A3BAZ2wsLd_nsI-VSxabYgA/view.

5. The template can be found at https://thinkingpathwayz .weebly.com/uploads/1/0/4/4/104440805/see_think_wonder_ template.pdf.

6. The template can be found at https://drive.google.com/file/d/ 1OTZpqDsWFyN29IfdmPVYUiG-AOVFuV8h/view.

7. Further details can be found at https://www.nextgenscience.org/ pe/5-ess1-2-earths-place-universe#:~:text=Students%20who% 20demonstrate%20understanding%20can,stars%20in%20 the%20night%20sky.

8. Further details can be found at https://danielsongroup.org/ framework/.

9. This template can be found at https://docs.google.com/ presentation/d/1x0k3FEI0zYmjYDP3Ap633FPQs4iPTjrBax25 OoKYkgM/edit#slide=id.g2011397ef82_0_28.

10. Zeph's work can be found at https://drive.google.com/drive/ folders/1Knis3Ru8fXrUMbPS-MAI-VkKPEfEyBIc.

11. These infographics can be found at https://drive.google.com/file/ d/1-hrN1sruu9Mi2HGkp6G9WsJiSQkyFjSM/view.

12. Further details can be found at https://mgiep.unesco.org/ iseeareport.

Chapter 7

Teachers and Leaders

Teaching is not just about imparting information to students – it is a journey that involves understanding how the brain learns. Educators who understand this notion act as mentors and facilitators, equipped with the tools to guide students to long-lasting understanding.[1]

Dr. Erika Galea

I have had the honor of working with several schools who have embraced the science of learning. On the following pages, I am highlighting a few of the teachers, leaders, and instructional coaches, with whom I have worked, who have gone beyond "just imparting information to students" and have incorporated evidence-informed strategies in guiding their students, and teachers, to long-lasting understanding.

STEPHANIE BURNS

Organization: Genesee Valley BOCES (Boards of Cooperative Educational Services), LeRoy, New York, USA

X (formerly Twitter): @stephburns420

How are evidence-informed teaching and learning used in your school and/or district?

The department/service that I manage supports the 22 component school districts with their professional learning needs. As a result, we pride ourselves on providing regional staff with evidence-informed teaching and learning practices that are an integral part of their continuous improvement efforts. As professional learning providers, we also utilize evidence-informed teaching techniques when working with participants. We make a conscious effort to be modeling those practices that we preach.

How is the science of learning incorporated into professional development?

Our department has worked very hard over the last four years to bring the science of learning (SOL) to the Genesee Valley BOCES region. We have conducted book studies on *Powerful Teaching*, brought in Patrice Bain as a featured speaker, and spent our regional curriculum council meeting learning about SOL. Our team has also incorporated SOL into our content cohort groups with teaching staff. We have engaged Teacher Sprints (Plan, Do, Study, Act) cycles with cohort teachers to implement SOL into their classrooms. SOL also emerged at our yearly Leadership Institute event to ensure administrators understand the importance of these practices on student achievement.

Patrice's note: I presented to the faculty at Genesee Valley BOCES in 2022 and worked directly with Stephanie Burns.

My trip to LeRoy, New York, was eventful. LeRoy is in upstate New York and the event was planned for the winter months. I usually fly but decided to drive instead. I got about half way (about six hours in) and Stephanie called me. A huge snowstorm was coming and they had to cancel my presentation. While turning around to go home, a big snowstorm was heading my way. I made it safely home. However, both Genesee and St. Louis were snowed in for days. We rescheduled for early summer and working with the dedicated Genesee faculty was well worth the wait.

KRISTIN DALEY CONTI

Grade level taught: 7

Subject: Science

years teaching: 25

School: Tantasqua Regional Junior High School

Location: Fiskdale, Massachusetts, USA

X (formerly Twitter): @daleyscience

How did you become interested in the science of teaching and learning? Describe your path to evidence-informed teaching.

I have been teaching middle school science for 25 years. I love reading and connecting with other educators to improve my practice. I initially became interested in the science of teaching and learning after seeing Pooja and Patrice on Matt Miller's Ditch Summit. The ideas behind retrieval practice, spacing, and interleaving really resonated with me and I immediately started using these practices within my classroom. I also provided resources about these strategies to both parents and students in my classes. When I was a student in middle school and high school, I did well without really learning how to study, but when I went to college, I really struggled. Because of this, I really want my students to move forward through school (and life), with not only the skills for being able to recall information, but also a little bit about how their brains work to make connections. I find the science of teaching and learning so interesting and valuable!

Strategy: Retrieval Guide – One Pager[2]

How do you use this strategy?

This strategy is used toward the end of a unit. It pairs with the study guide that I provide, but this "one pager" has students retrieving important information from our current unit. I created categories such as: something to remember, real-world connections, important facts, vocab, and a spot for sketchnotes. I do not tell students what to put in each box, so in the end, everyone's work is slightly different. Students can collaborate and discuss the recalled information, and prompts can be given to those students who need some scaffolding.

Power Tools used:

Retrieval, Spacing, Metacognition

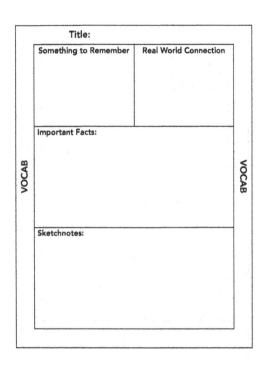

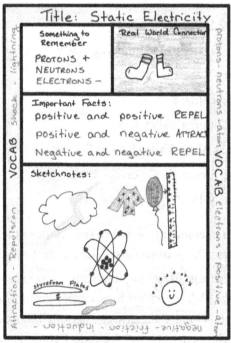

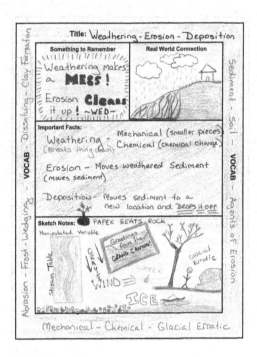

EMMA DEHNER

Grade level taught: 3rd grade, ages 8–9

Subjects: All

years teaching: 8

School: Thunder Valley K–8

District: St. Vrain Valley School District

Location: Frederick, Colorado, USA

X (formerly Twitter): @MrsDehner

How did you become interested in the science of teaching and learning? Describe your path to evidence-informed teaching.

When I first began teaching, I quickly realized how interested I was in the "Why" behind how we present information and the science behind the learning that our brains do. I found discrepancies in the way we, as a collective, taught and the way that brains learned. My goal is and has always been to meet students where they are and present information in the best possible way for them to retain the information.

Strategy: Question Jar

How do you use this strategy?

In Social Studies, specifically, we place vocabulary and concepts into a Question Jar. Thus, there is content from every unit. I have a sound board that plays, "Do You Remember?"[3] When the music plays, we draw three questions. Students answer the questions and then we discuss.

Power Tools used:

Retrieval, Spacing, Interleaving, Metacognition

HEATHER ELLIS

Grade level taught: 8 (really 6, 7, 8 – we loop up with our students)

Subjects: Social Studies, US History

years teaching: 20

School: Westview Middle School

District: St. Vrain Valley School District

Location: Longmont, Colorado, USA

X (formerly Twitter): @HeatherLea303

How did you become interested in the science of teaching and learning? Describe your path to evidence-informed teaching.

I first started reading books about the science of learning like *Neuroteach*[4] and *Make It Stick*,[5] because it just made sense to learn more about how we learn. Then in 2019, I was part of the first Science of Learning Collaborative in my district and I'm so grateful for that experience. It was a very mixed group of teachers from different grade levels and subjects. We read *Powerful Teaching*[6] together and shared out all the ways we were implementing retrieval practice, spacing, interleaving, metacognition, and feedback in our classrooms. I learned so much from that group and it completely changed my practice to the benefit of my students. Yes, I rejoice at overall higher test scores, but the best part has been when students come back to visit and tell me how they make retrieval notes and use self-quizzing, and even make their own "brain blasts" because they see how much those strategies really help in their high school advanced placement (AP) courses. It's exciting when students really learn how they learn.

Strategy: Vertical Conversations (adapted from *Thinking Classrooms*)

How do you use this strategy?

One of my goals this year has been to promote academic oracy, particularly for my ELL (English Language Learner) students, but really just for all my students in low-stakes ways. I have an extra challenge of very large class sizes (60+ middle school students), so traditional small group discussion or stations are extra challenging to manage. When I came across Peter Liljedahl's *Thinking Classrooms*, I thought using vertical white-boards to facilitate small group discussions might just work. A couple times a week, I split students up into groups of three and usually give them a retrieval/interleaving type task. For example, "Make a diagram that shows the three branches of government and the checks and balances each has over the others." Students have a couple of minutes to silently think about the question, then they are randomly grouped and work together to talk about and complete the task. So many of the retrieval, spacing, and interleaving type tasks that used to be individual or collaborative via a digital discussion (silent) are now talking activities. Sometimes, I give my ELL students sentence stems or a word bank, but often they would rather just dive in and try, which is exactly what I was hoping for.

Power Tools used:

Retrieval, Spacing, Interleaving, Metacognition

Ideas for Retrieval Practice in the Secondary Classroom is an ever-growing document I put together with my friend Janis Vogelsberg.[7] It has ideas and many modifications for online school, since we had to quickly switch gears in March 2020. You'll notice many of the ideas are from *Powerful Teaching*.

Look at the picture of students working on either side of a whiteboard to answer review questions for the unit.

AMY ERDMAN

Role: Instructional Coach

Grade level taught: 5th grade, age 10–11

Subjects: All

years teaching: 21

District: St. Vrain Valley School District

Location: Longmont, Colorado, USA

X (formerly Twitter): @erdfive

How did you become interested in the science of teaching and learning? Describe your path to evidence-informed teaching.

I was offered to join a group of educators to investigate how students learn. The group was led by Kim Wiggins (a former member of our assessment department). While in this group, we read research papers as well as *Powerful Teaching*. Since the information and practices made a huge change in our classrooms, we brought in Patrice Bain for a day of professional development.

Strategies: Retrieval/Metacognition and Analysis of Math Test, why mistakes were made+

How do you use this strategy?

At the beginning of the day, students are given four problems on various topics that were already taught in math. This procedure ensures that students do not forget material that was taught earlier in the year.

Power Tools used:

Retrieval, Metacognition

Example of **Retrieval/Metacognition.**

Retrieval

1.	2.
3.	4.

Example of the **Analysis of a Math Test.**

Topic 1 Assessment Reflection				
Question	Correct	Incorrect	Skill	Error Analysis (why incorrect)
1			Expressions equal to number X power of 10	
2			Identify correct standard form	
3			Identify digit that is 1/10 value of the other	
4A			Identify decimal that falls between 2 values	
4B			Identify all equivalent decimals of a model	
5			Identify correct explanation of how to compare 2 decimals	
6A			Identify next 2 numbers in pattern	
6B			Recognize each term is 10 times greater	
7A			Round to the nearest hundredth	

How are evidence-informed teaching and learning used in your school and/or district?

In my district, there are many teachers who have studied *Powerful Teaching* tools and incorporate the practices in their classrooms. In addition, the district offers professional development on the science of learning.

How is the science of learning incorporated into coaching?

When coaching, I have teachers reflect on how a lesson went and decide next steps for teaching. I also plan with teachers to incorporate retrieval practices for all subjects. In addition, I model interleaving during a lesson, since elementary teachers teach all subjects.

An example of **My Reflections** is shown in table format.

My Reflections

My Strengths	
My Opportunities for Growth	
My Plan for Improvement	
The Evidence I Will Use to Demonstrate My Growth	

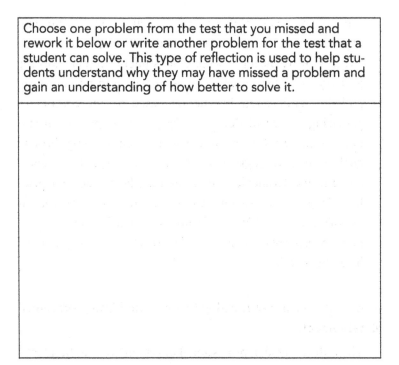

Choose one problem from the test that you missed and rework it below or write another problem for the test that a student can solve. This type of reflection is used to help students understand why they may have missed a problem and gain an understanding of how better to solve it.

SUZANNAH EVANS

District: St. Vrain Valley School District

Location: Longmont, Colorado, USA

X (formerly Twitter): @SuzannahEvans2

How are evidence-informed teaching and learning used in your school and/or district?

We believe seeking out the most recent cognitive research and using an Instructional Framework[8] grounded in continuous analysis and reflection is the key to propelling student success. *What is the evidence of learning taking place?* is the question we constantly ask ourselves as educators and inspire our students to ask of themselves as well. Understanding and objectively analyzing our data, whether formative or summative, is how we meet the needs of all students in their learning journey. We intentionally plan next steps, and refine, adjust, and differentiate our instruction based on the continuous gathering and evaluation of evidence. We empower our students to be self-directed and evaluate their learning through goal setting and progress monitoring, building self-awareness and efficacy. To enable students and teachers to activate prior knowledge, apply learning to new content, see obstacles as opportunities, and utilize feedback and reflection for progress, consistent evidence-based instructional strategies must be embedded.

How is the science of learning incorporated into professional development?

The ultimate goal of professional development is to build efficacy and capacity in educators that will positively affect and improve the learning of students. Embedding research-based cognitive strategies in our staff development to activate prior learning, digest new material, and reflect is the first step in modeling how those practices can be transferred to the classroom. Beyond the embedding of these practices, we also intentionally create transparency around their identification and purpose. Best practices in learning and instruction should not be viewed as secretive or magical. True empowerment of our educators comes from giving them the keys to analyzing their own learning, setting goals, and continuously achieving growth. Furthermore, seeking to understand how we engage in learning as adults is content-agnostic and therefore applicable for all teachers as they take practices and new learning back to their students.

HANNAH FELDMAN

School: Yellow Springs Elementary School

District: Frederick County Public Schools

Location: Frederick, Maryland, USA

X (formerly Twitter): @MrsFeldmanFCPS

How are evidence-informed teaching and learning used in your school and/or district?

At Yellow Springs Elementary we use a unique block during the day called SPARK to accelerate student learning using evidence-informed strategies. The SPARK block is a 30-minute period, 4 days a week where two additional staff members (interventionists, specialists, etc.) join the grade-level team to further reduce the teacher-to-student ratio. Students are regrouped homogeneously based on a preassessment of the targeted priority standard to be taught a month or two in the future. A SPARK rotation lasts 5 weeks. During the SPARK block, teachers preteach the priority standard based on the students' prior knowledge as indicated on the preassessment. The focus is on connecting foundational skills the students already know to the new content standards, specifically targeting vocabulary. This method provides interleaving and spacing so that students are primed for the priority standard learning. When the priority standard is eventually taught during the regular class period, the use of retrieval practice happens naturally. We have found great success with this acceleration model over the last two years.

How is the science of learning incorporated into professional development?

The science of learning has been a focus of Yellow Springs Elementary professional development over the last two years.

We have examined how students learn and retain information through faculty meetings and SPARK planning sessions. Specific strategies are shared during these times together. When my Assistant Principal and I observe teachers, we look for these strategies and provide feedback on the effectiveness of their implementation. Several members of our staff are also working with Deans for Impact and Hood College in a Learning Science Consortium on Effortful Thinking. They have been sharing their learning with their teams and we intend to have them share with the full faculty at the conclusion of the year.

CONNIE FINK, ANNA CLAIRE McKAY

Grade level taught: Fink, 5th-grade Social Studies; McKay, Middle School Learning Coordinator

years teaching: Fink, 18; McKay, in education 30 years

School: University School of Nashville

Location: Nashville, Tennessee, USA

LinkedIn: connie-lópez-fink-6985b066

How did you become interested in the science of teaching and learning? Describe your path to evidence-informed teaching.

Connie and Anna Claire have always been curious about the intricacies of the learning process and sharing it with our middle-school students. In particular, we strive to equip students with an informal toolbox of learning strategies and habits that will last them well beyond their middle-school years. We truly caught the "MBE bug" (Mind Brain Education) at the *Learning and the Brain* conference in Boston, Massachusetts, in 2019. Through Connie's lens of social studies teacher and Anna Claire's lens of meeting the needs of diverse learners, we've begun to create a curriculum to empower ALL students with the science of learning while also learning about the history of our nation. Attending ResearchED [conferences] and visiting the CTTL (The Center for Transformative Teaching and Learning) and Frederick County Public Schools (Maryland, USA) has fueled our continued growth and implementation. We are working to "spread the word." Connie mentors teachers across the U.S. with science-informed practices and Anna Claire weaves MBE into her interactions with students and parents across all middle-school grade levels and subject areas.

Strategy: Powerful Partnership and the ME-J!

How do you use this strategy?

Connie and Anna Claire's partnership feels like its own type of "Power Tool." It allows us to create a culture where retrieval practice, metacognition, interleaving, and spacing are the norm. Anna Claire teaches in Connie's room multiple times a year, providing factual information about how a memory is formed, traits of the adolescent brain, and strategies for making long-term memories. On a *daily* basis, Connie weaves Power Tools and concepts like myelination and neuroplasticity into social studies learning. Our "ME-J" (Memory Effort Journal) is one retrieval tool we use that interleaves social studies and MBE content and spaces it out over time!

Power Tools used:

Retrieval, Spacing, Interleaving, Metacognition

The "Memory Effort Journal" aka ME-J! We use the ME-J to support the use of all four Power Tools!

Cover

Retrieval Practice Choice Board

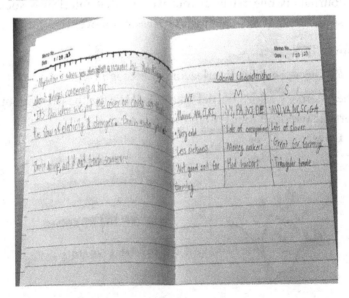

MBE Retrieval

Social Studies Retrieval

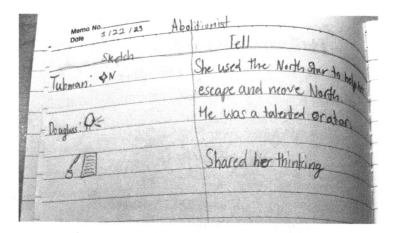

Developing metacognition by coding what we know and what was added.

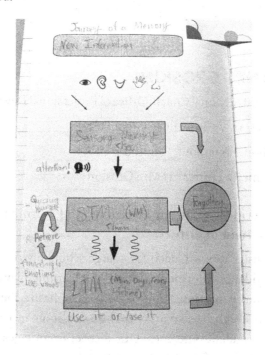

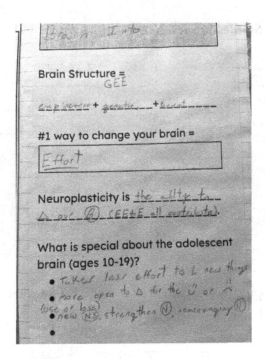

COURTNEY GROSKIN

Role: Instructional Coach, Office of Professional Development

District: St. Vrain Valley School District

Location: Longmont, Colorado, USA

X (formerly Twitter): @MissGroskin

How are evidence-informed teaching and learning used in your school and/or district?

As an Instructional Coach for a large school district in Colorado, evidence-informed teaching and learning play a crucial role in our educational approach. We emphasize the integration of research-backed practices into classroom instruction to enhance student outcomes. Our district encourages teachers to stay abreast of the latest educational research and leverage evidence-based strategies that have been proven to be effective.

We offer professional development courses around *Powerful Teaching, The Thinking Classroom, Thinking Maps,* etc.

Professional development sessions are designed to provide teachers with the tools and knowledge needed to incorporate evidence-informed practices into their teaching. This includes workshops on utilizing data-driven instruction, implementing research-based instructional strategies, and staying informed about advancements in educational research.

Additionally, collaborative platforms and regular meetings are established to facilitate discussions among educators, fostering a culture of continuous learning. We hold regular Professional Learning Community (PLC) meetings at each building. Teachers are encouraged to share successful strategies and experiences, creating a dynamic environment where evidence-informed practices can be disseminated and adopted.

Our district also invests in resources and technology that align with evidence-based teaching approaches, ensuring that teachers have access to tools that support their implementation. We have a 1:1 student iPad initiative. By promoting evidence-informed teaching and learning, we aim to cultivate a learning environment that is not only responsive to the diverse needs of our students but is also founded on the latest research to drive educational excellence.

BLAKE HARVARD

Grade level taught: 9th–12th grade

Subject: AP Psychology

years teaching: 18

School: James Clemens High School

District: Madison City Schools

Location: Madison, Alabama, USA

X (formerly Twitter)/LinkedIn: @effortfuleduktr

How did you become interested in the science of teaching and learning? Describe your path to evidence-informed teaching.

Approximately seven years ago, I stumbled upon The Learning Scientists on Twitter [now X]. I loved how succinctly and clearly they wrote about why and how to use learning strategies. It just made so much sense to use what research has indicated works better in the classroom to instruct and educate students. From that point to today, I've tried to learn as much as I can via research on retrieval practice, spaced practice, etc. to improve instruction and learning in my classroom.

Strategy: Brain – Book – Buddy

How do you use this strategy?

I apply this strategy whenever I am assessing student learning. It is great, because it is not tied to the type of material being assessed or the type of questions being assessed. It asks students to first read through the material and use only their brain to answer questions . . . no cheating by using other sources for answers. This tells them what they really know. Then, they can go through the assessment using their notebook or textbook. Then, finally they can turn to a buddy and check answers and fill in any information they still don't know. A much broader explanation of this can be found in The Effortful Educator.[9] [A useful graphic of the strategy is also available.[10]]

Power Tools used:

Retrieval, Spacing, Metacognition

Brain - Book - Buddy

Make any assessment more impactful.

Three steps to follow.

1	**2**	**3**
Use your brain to answer	Use your notebook or textbook to answer	Use your buddies to answer
Highlight answers in orange	Highlight answers in blue	Highlight answers in yellow

Questions to consider:
1. How many were answered correctly using only your brain?
2. Why did you answer the other questions incorrectly?
3. How will this inform and tailor future studies of this material?

effortfuleducator.com

THE EFFORTFUL EDUCATOR
APPLYING COGNITIVE PSYCHOLOGY TO THE CLASSROOM

@effortfuleduktr

AMBER HAVEN

Grade level taught: 5th grade, age 10

Subjects: Writing, Reading, and Science

years teaching: 15

School: Columbia Middle School

District: Columbia Community District #4

Location: Columbia, Illinois, USA

How did you become interested in the science of teaching and learning? Describe your path to evidence-informed teaching.

I attended a workshop many years ago where I heard about the Power Tools and how to implement them into my classroom. Since that workshop, I have incorporated retrieval practice, spacing, interleaving, and feedback-driven metacognition on a daily basis. I continue to search for ways to integrate these Power Tools into each lesson, as I have seen, firsthand, the benefits the tools have for student success.

Strategy: Fill-in-the-blank Speaking

How do you use this strategy?

During the beginning of the school year, one routine that I teach my students involves them knowing how to respond to me when my hands are held in different positions.

For example, when my hands are on my shoulders, students know that I am the only one speaking. When my hands point to my head, students know that when I ask a question, they are only supposed to think about their answer rather than state it out loud.

When my hand is in the air, students know that I would like volunteers to answer the question that I am about to ask. When I make a circular motion with my hand, the students know that I would like them to pair and share.

Finally, when my hands move from my shoulders and point them out to the class, students know that they should respond chorally to my next question.

With this routine in place, I hardly ever finish a sentence without gesturing. Students are actively engaged because they are constantly watching how to respond. I change the methods for responding frequently and interchangeably.

I am able to ask questions from previous lessons that tie into the current lesson because the students already know the answer. Asking students to constantly retrieve learned information is a low-stakes method of formative assessment. Additionally, I ask students to repeat concepts and vocabulary that I taught that same class period. Doing so brings new concepts to the front of students' minds and keeps them actively sorting through new and old information.

In the example below, I have typed a 5–10-minute review and connect segment from one of my science classes. Every time you see a _____, that means I am gesturing. With retrievals such as this one, I usually gesture for a choral response. You will see the expected answer from students in the parentheses. As I listen to the students respond chorally, I watch for their mouths to be forming the correct answer. I use this as a formative assessment. If I see a student who is not answering, I am able to assess and decide if they are choosing not to participate, I can notice if they are feeling "down" and having a bad day, or I can see that they do not know the information. (I also tell students this . . . I explain that I am watching their mouths move by saying the correct answer so that I know where their skills are. I also explain to students that if they only mouth the words instead of saying them loudly, that is okay.)

Example

I teach the terms "producer, herbivore, omnivore, and carnivore." The next day, I teach the terms "primary, secondary, and tertiary consumer."

To start the class, students draw a food web and label the producer, herbivore, and omnivore to retrieve the information learned the previous day. This is reviewed as a class and correct answers are verified.

During the review, I will say:

Looking at the food chain on the whiteboard, the grass is the _____ (producer).

And producers are the important key to the food chain because they transform solar _____ (energy) into _____ (glucose). Oh! That's a cool word!

Can you all tell me the chemical formula for glucose? _____ ($C_6H_{12}O_6$, sung to a beat that we've practiced). Nice!

Okay, so the _____ (producer) changes solar energy to chemical energy through a process that starts with a p. . . _____ (photosynthesis, singing the word to the tune we learned before). Yes!

Now that we have glucose _____ ($C_6H_{12}O_6$), our first consumer can get its energy from it!

A consuuuuuuuuumer takes in its _____ (foooooooooooood for energy!).

What is the name of this first consumer? _____ (an herbivore!). Yes. Now that herbivore passes its energy from the grass to the next consumer. What type of consumer is this fox? _____ (an omnivore). Yes!

What types of food does an omnivore eat? _____ (plants and meat/other animals!). Excellent. Do you see how I connect the organisms within this food chain? Do you see that I have arrows pointing from one organism to another? Look at the direction of these arrows. Now check the direction of your arrows on your paper.

Class, what do arrows show? _____ (arrows show the energy flow, chanted with the rhythm learned previously). Yes! So, these arrows are showing the energy passing through the ecosystem from creature to creature [this is the definition of a food chain, so I plugged this in here for good measure]. The energy from the grass has finally made its way to the coyote! What type of consumer is a coyote? _____ (carnivore).

What you've just read takes a tiny amount of time, yet it engages all students, it retrieves information from the day before, the week before, the month before, and beyond. It is low stakes because there is no grade attached, and students can verify their answers among their peers. I make sure to repeat the terms throughout.

The fill-in-the-blank review is in case a student is having difficulty sorting through the vocabulary. Repeated exposure and repeated opportunity to retrieve the concepts has proven to be very helpful.

I conduct a fill-in-the-blank review daily. It has now become routine for my students and for me, and we are able to get through reviewing material very quickly. In fact, students can easily provide word-for-word definitions for me in April that they learned in August because of the frequent, low-stakes, retrieval practice.

Power Tools used:

Retrieval, Spacing, Interleaving, Metacognition

Strategy: Indirect Vocabulary Instruction

How do you use this strategy?

I am very purposeful with the vocabulary I use in my instruction. For example, in 5th-grade writing, students will write a five-paragraph expository, explanatory essay during the third quarter. Because of the complexity of these terms, I use the words routinely from the first month of school. Anytime something is informational, whether it be in writing class, reading class, or science class, I use a form of "expository" or "explanatory." Because of this, when we reach the essay unit, students already have been exposed to the term and do not feel intimidated by it. Another example of using indirect vocabulary instruction is in my science class. Every day, my science students record the daily weather. They record data such as: current temperature, feels like temperature, dew point, air pressure, humidity, wind speed, moon phase, and the sunset/sunrise. Exposing students to these terms every day and having them study them from the beginning of the year has allowed them to analyze and make predictions and theories regarding the world around them by December. Due to the observations of the sunset/sunrise, students make connections on their own regarding the earth's revolution around the sun impacting the length of our day. Students already know about the impact of air pressure when we get to our atmospheric unit in April. Students can start converting Fahrenheit temperature to Celsius because they are experiencing the temperatures on a daily basis. Students know the difference between weather and climate based on the long-term observations and the short-term measurements. By presenting the daily weather report as common language, students are able to hold meaningful, mature conversations with other students and with adults. They incorporate "inches of Mercury" into their daily vocabulary when referring to air pressure. The things these kids are capable of just because of the repeated exposure and retrieval is so inspiring.

The students are so comfortable with the terminology because they are used to it. They record it. They present it. They share it with each other. By the time we get to the specific units that study the concepts, we get to dig deeper much faster than we would if I needed to teach the terms within the unit.

Power Tools used:

Retrieval, Spacing, Interleaving, Metacognition

LEAH KUNTZ

Grade level taught: 8th grade

Subject: Language Arts

years teaching: 24

School: Timberline PK-8

District: St. Vrain Valley School District

Location: Longmont, Colorado, USA

How did you become interested in the science of teaching and learning? Describe your path to evidence-informed teaching.

In my 24 years teaching elementary and middle school, I've noticed students struggling to retain concepts and take ownership of their learning. Eager to improve, I embarked on a journey to address this issue. In 2019, I discovered *Powerful Teaching: Unleash the Science of Learning* by Pooja K. Agarwal and Patrice M. Bain. Immersed in its teachings that summer, I integrated evidence-based practices like retrieval, spacing, interleaving, and metacognition into my lesson plans for the new school year. Embracing the mindset that teaching is about fostering critical thinking and problem-solving in students, not just imparting knowledge, I witnessed remarkable results. My confidence in teaching soared, and my students became more engaged learners. This transformative experience underscores the profound impact of implementing proven methods to enhance student retention and agency.

Strategies: Two Things Retrieval and Brain Dumps

How do you use this strategy?

In my 8th-grade classroom, students engage in a Two Things retrieval strategy following independent reading sessions. During the first 10–15 minutes of class, they select either a personal choice book or our current novel study and record two key insights from their reading. Additionally, every month, students are tasked with recalling and discussing two points from each topic we cover, whether individually, in small groups, or with a partner.

One of my favorite activities for vocabulary retrieval is the "brain dump," where students explore and retrieve new words encountered in their reading. This practice significantly contributes to their literacy and oral communication development. Observing my students engaging in (domain-specific and academic) language discussions during these activities is inspiring and fulfilling.

Power Tools used:

Retrieval, Spacing, Interleaving

Template: **SELF – NOTES – BUDDY**

NAME_____ CORE_____

TOPIC	TWO THINGS RETRIEVAL

Student work examples from February Retrieval Practice using Self – Notes – Buddy. All of the QR codes supplied by Leah Kuntz:

Other EXAMPLES of strategies:

Vocabulary Dump (15/20 Words!!)

Two Things Independent Reading Retrieval

SAMANTHA LAFEVER

Grade level taught: 4th grade, age 9–10

Subjects: All

years teaching: 5

School: Mead Elementary

District: St. Vrain Valley School District

Location: Mead, Colorado, USA

How did you become interested in the science of teaching and learning? Describe your path to evidence-informed teaching.

I've always been drawn to metacognitive thinking, often engaging in introspective analysis. In college, I faced my social fears by delving into Public Speaking courses and public deliberation, learning context-variable coping strategies. I continue to refine my thinking iteratively, targeting areas for growth, refinement, or overhaul. Recently, I've become more aware that not everyone finds this approach as accessible or comfortable. While I take discomfort as a catalyst for personal growth, others may throw up mental barriers. In my twenties, I moved from emergency management and startups into teaching. I brought a unique perspective to preparing students for the pace of workplace pivots. This journey led me to explore the science of teaching and learning, engaging teacher research and implementing pedagogical concepts with an eye on outcomes. I feel that there is a powerful symbiotic relationship between scholarly inquiry and personal development. This ongoing pursuit not only captivates my own intellectual curiosity, yielding gratifying outcomes for me, but also for my students as they aim toward becoming adaptable learners in the world. I involve them in every iteration I undertake in the classroom as stakeholders.

Strategy: Microinterleaving in Mathematics with Metacognitive Differentiation Toward Flexible Mastery

How do you use this strategy?

The foundation involves

A. emphasizing cognitive flexibility within curricular bounds, and

B. fostering self-awareness through a customized version of Jeff Nottingham's learning pit graphic, adapted by my peer, Nicole Schmidt.

The strategy guides students toward flexible mastery at their own pace by teaching from the curriculum, ensuring comprehension, and using quick assessments for clean data to prevent mimicry. Additionally, resources like Khan Academy expose students to varied visual representations, fostering metacognitive analysis as they differentiate between models. Ultimately, the objective is to empower students to independently apply mathematical principles to new tasks, transcending the curriculum's constraints and becoming adaptable learners. To support this, we implement spaced retrieval practices that incorporate evolving grades based on standards/skills throughout the year, reflecting the nonlinear nature of mastery.

Example

Here is an example of Ms. LaFever's reflection using the:

Retrieval/Metacognitive Crossover Check for Ms. LaFever's Classroom (BMES 4th) Originally created by: Shane Saeed, Tom Steele, Amanda White (2020).

Iteration 2: January 2020 (in person)

Develop Ideas: What are you going to implement?	OK, one piece of feedback I got is that the flux grades are relying on a feedback loop that didn't involve student reflection on the feedback. SO new plan is to give the retrieval practice earlier in the week and have them reflect on the results the next school day in a written form. This expands the feedback cycle to be: initial teaching, feedback, and grading, followed by weekly retrieval practice covering most previously covered topics, followed by next-day reflection on teacher evaluation/feedback on the retrieval quiz. The grade changes will reflect the cumulative outcome of BOTH days each week, as opposed to just the quiz. Quiz will now be from the Daily Common Core Review from enVision instead of Khan Academy for consistency . . . I like the custom retrieval but for trying to see overall trends it can be more difficult.
Attempt: Use it with your students.	Starting next week on 2/12/21 . . . so the schedule kind of looks something like this: 2/12/21 Retrieval quiz 2/13/21 Student reflection and resubmission 2/14–15/21 Grade/proficiency modification if needed
Reflect: How did it go? What went well? What didn't? What can I ask peers about for feedback?	This went really well and was a great extension that allowed us to get into feedback. The kids would attach reflections and requests for small group/ one-on-one work where kids can self-select their needed support. There were still four kids who needed assistance with this during this time.

Adapt: What are you going to keep? What are you going to tweak?	Alright, from here I also realized that the kids needed more flexible situations to utilize their skills in . . . enVision shows them in a fairly specific way. Question structure can become familiar, so I wanted to get back into Khan to give them two exposures to math problem presentation before Colorado Measures of Academic Success (CMAS).
Test: *How* impactful was it?	Quite! For the most part, the kids showed significant improvements in self-reflection that supported further mastery goals by getting them specific help they needed, which they identified, which showed (in over 80% of cases) higher performance over time in spaced as well as interleaved practice.

Power Tools used:

Retrieval, Spacing, Interleaving, Metacognition

THE LEAF TRUST

Location: South Gloucestershire, UK

How are evidence-informed teaching and learning used in your school and/or district?

We are a Trust of 13 primary schools with pupils ranging from age 4–11 based in South Gloucestershire, UK. Many of our schools were familiar with some of the main principles of cognitive science and had been working to employ strategies to, for example, reduce cognitive load, space practice, and promote retrieval, for several years. *Powerful Teaching*[11] provided a single point of reference for our teachers, reducing the range of areas to four and providing practical strategies which teachers could use in the classroom with minimal preparation. Following a training session for teaching staff in November 2023, teachers are currently experimenting with strategies such as Brain Dumps for retrieval. The feedback from teachers, after the session, was positive – they believe that the four Power Tools will enable them to extend and build upon the work they have conducted previously on evidence-informed practice.

How is the science of learning incorporated into professional development?

As mentioned above, we invested in a training session, facilitated by Patrice Bain, for all of our teachers in Years 2–6 (age 6–11). We felt the content of *Powerful Teaching* was most appropriate for these year groups. Our Trust's Head of Professional Development facilitated the session – Patrice prerecorded videos for us and then joined us for a live Q&A session. Prior to the day, we had provided all of our school's Deputy Headteachers with a copy of *Powerful Teaching* and had run some sessions with them about the content. This was done ahead of the main training session so that they could set the scene in school and support staff effectively after the training. It also meant that each school could meet the content at a point they felt ready for (e.g. some schools were further ahead than others in their application of cognitive science principles). We are hopeful our approach will maximize success.

CHAD LEMONS

Grade level taught: K–5, ages 5–10

Subject: Music

years teaching: 14

School: Mead Elementary

District: St. Vrain Valley School District

Location: Mead, Colorado, USA

X (formerly Twitter): @ChadTLemons

How did you become interested in the science of teaching and learning? Describe your path to evidence-informed teaching.

Shane Saeed and Suzy Evans interviewed Patrice Bain on an episode of the VrainWaves Podcast and I was absolutely hooked. The podcast was inspiring and gave me such a surge of energy to utilize the strategies being discussed in my own classroom. The entire episode was upbeat, positive, and I found myself smiling and laughing along with them.

Patrice's words to her students, "I'm going to teach you how to learn," left such an impression on me. I've always had the mindset that I'm a music teacher, but now I find myself driven to teach my students how to learn, and my vehicle just happens to be the music classroom.

A mentor of mine often said, "Music is like life; it is far too serious to take so seriously." The science of learning tools helped me apply evidence-informed teaching while simultaneously structuring lessons that are playful, experiential, and meaningful for the students.

Strategy: Music Vocabulary Playbook

How do you use this strategy?

I developed the Music Vocabulary Playbook to be a playful game that borrows a few concepts from American football and gets the students retrieving music vocabulary, translations of Italian definitions, and interleaves dynamic (volume) levels with tempo (speed). I was thrilled to see students who are usually less enthusiastic about music fully engaging with this game.

Students work in teams to memorize a "playbook" of music vocabulary words in Italian and their definition in English. The game begins with a brain dump for teams to produce as many words as possible before receiving the playbook for review. Our specials rotation revolves on a pace that organically utilizes spacing. Each round, select students from both teams join the teacher in the huddle to receive a "play" in Italian. Teams work quickly to retrieve (from memory) the English translation, or receive help from teammates when needed, and race to write the translation on the whiteboard.

Power Tools used:

Retrieval, Spacing, Interleaving

CHERYL LOTT

School: Albert Village Community Primary School

Location: Derbyshire, East Midlands, UK

X (formerly Twitter): @CP_Dclasstalk

How are evidence-informed teaching and learning used in your school and/or district?

Using evidence-led approaches to teaching is key at Albert Village. This includes key texts/pieces of research. These include: *Powerful Teaching*,[12] the Learning Scientists, Rosenshine's "Principles of Instruction," Dunlosky's "Strengthening the Student Toolbox," Sherrington's WalkThrus, Cognitive Load Theory and Dual Coding. We do lots using the Leitner Method and this is currently a huge focus that we are developing a variety of programs around. In tandem with this I am working to translate how children learn/what we do here with parents in a digestible, practical way so that we can harness the lever of parental participation in order to improve outcomes for our children. The golden triangle! We lead parent/carer "workingshops" with the children present and teacher modeling key strategies so that parents feel less under pressure and informed. Teaching how to learn is a golden thread.

How is the science of learning incorporated into professional development?

High-quality continuing professional development (CPD) is fundamental to our school. For over a decade now we have used the Science of Learning to ensure our practitioners are empowered. Teachers and support staff receive regular professional development through both Trust- and School-based practitioners. We are also the hub in East Midlands for the Chartered College which has brought up the benefits of many educational expert speakers from the UK and beyond. We follow Education Endowment Federation recommendations for CPD, ensuring that teachers: build knowledge, are motivated, develop techniques, and embed practice. This is done in a collaborative and supportive way and teachers receive bespoke incremental coaching and subject-lead support. A backbone of our practice to maximize the impact of "the science of learning" is New Zealand's Professor Rubie-Davies's "High Expectations Teaching," having been fortunate to work with her at the school.

DEEPIKA NARULA

Grade level taught: Year 7 to Year 13 (UK)

Subject: Chemistry

years teaching: 11

School: St. Albans School

District: Hertfordshire

Location: St. Albans, UK

X (formerly Twitter): @MrsDNarula

How did you become interested in the science of teaching and learning? Describe your path to evidence-informed teaching.

My journey toward the science of teaching and learning started through the Chartered Teacher course. During this course, I learned about the importance of cognitive science in education. After reading books like *Powerful Teaching*[13] by Agarwal and Bain and *Retrieval Practice*[14] by Kate Jones, I realised what my teaching practice lacked. Science of learning provided answers to many questions like why students don't perform well in the tests and why they forget learning so easily. It fine-tuned my teaching and allowed me to think deeply about my explanations, marking, testing, and even having conversations with pupils and their parents. The biggest impact was that I was able to suggest how my students could improve their revision techniques. I became confident in having conversations with colleagues and became a responsive teacher. Along with the positives, there were a few setbacks, and with reflection, I adapted how the science of learning could be practically applied in the classroom.

Strategy: Feedback-driven Metacognition and Retrieval

How do you use this strategy?

Powerful Teaching[15] gave me inspiration about feedback-driven metacognition and I have used it as given in the book as part of a project during CTeach. After the project, I adapted it and used it as retrieval practice along with carousel quizzes in my lessons. I pick three questions on the carousel and ask students to put a* or ? if they know the answer, then they attempt it followed by a discussion around the answers they have got right or wrong. Students are prompted with further discussion to reflect on where they have gone wrong and why. Low-ability students have found this strategy useful as they could know their weaknesses easily.

Power Tools used:

Retrieval, Metacognition

Examples:

Q. No.	*/?	Question	Answer
1		Unit of concentration	
2		$5cm^3$ to dm^3	
3		Formula to calculate concentration	
4		Number of moles in $5cm^3$ of NaOH solution	
5		Concentration of 0.987 moles of 10 cm^3HCl	

	*/?	
1.		Calcium reacts with oxygen to form calcium oxide. Write down the word equation, balanced symbol equation with state symbols.
2.		40g of calcium reacts with oxygen to form 56g of calcium oxide. How much oxygen does it react with?
3.		In question 2, find the simplest whole number ratio to balance the equation.
4.		If 32g of oxygen reacts with excess of calcium, how much calcium oxide is formed?

Ionic Compound (Name)	Ionic Formula	Working Out	Name:
Sodium chloride			
Magnesium oxide			
Lithium oxide			
Copper (II) chloride			
Calcium oxide			
Magnesium sulphate			
Aluminium oxide			
Calcium hydroxide			
Potassium sulphate			

Nailed it   Almost there   Got it   What can I do to improve?

Name-   Class-   Formula of ions and compounds under 3 minutes

1. Hydrogen Ion	1.		1. Hydrogen Ion	1.	
2. Hydroxide Ion	2.		2. Bromide Ion	2.	
3. Nitrate Ion	3.		3. Magnesium Ion	3.	
4. Lithium Ion	4.		4. Sulphide Ion	4.	
5. Bromide Ion	5.		5. Zinc Ion	5.	
6. Zinc Ion	6.		6. Sulphate	6.	
7. Sulphide Ion	7.		7. Sodium Ion	7.	
8. Carbonate Ion	8.		8. Chloride Ion	8.	
9. Sulphate Ion	9.		9. Barium Ion	9.	
10. Potassium Ion	10.		10. Hydroxide Ion	10.	
11. Lithium Hydroxide	11.		11. Sulphuric Acid	11.	
12. Lithium Oxide	12.		12. Zinc Bromide	12.	
13. Lithium Sulphide	13.		13. Zinc Hydroxide	13.	
14. Lithium Bromide	14.		14. Zinc Chloride	14.	
15. Zinc Oxide	15.		15. Zinc Sulphate	15.	

Nailed it	Not Yet

Nailed it	Not Yet

COURTNEY OSTAFF

Grade level taught: Grades 5–12 (homeschooling K–12)

Subjects: Math, Science, Social Studies (English language arts)

years teaching: K–12: 10, Post-secondary: 6

School: Well-trained Mind Academy; homeschool

District: Private school and my homeschool

Location: Online school and my home

How did you become interested in the science of teaching and learning? Describe your path to evidence-informed teaching.

I first became interested in evidence-based education when my eldest child was learning to read, and I realized that the preschool deliberately did not teach letter-sound correspondence. The teacher told me that if I was interested in having her learn how to read with that method, then I needed to do it myself at home. I didn't know how to do that, so I picked up a lot of books about how people learn to read, and then from there, branched out into using that information in my professional work. I was lucky enough to be assigned to teach a curriculum that had interleaved, interval-spaced retrieval practice already built into it, and I could see how powerful it was for student learning. Not always easy, but producing lasting learning gains.

Strategy: Yearly Planning – Creating Your Own Pacing Guide

How do you use this strategy?

Every year, both for my homeschool and for my professional teaching, I create a pacing guide. This helps me decide what specific topics I want to teach and how long I want to spend on a given topic. This allows me to schedule retrieval practice, interval spacing, interleaving, and metacognition into my teaching. Often, I include this in my syllabus, so that parents are aware of what we're studying, when we're studying it, and the expected assignments in any given week. In my homeschool, this task translates to a daily lesson checklist. In both cases, this pacing guide helps students with executive function issues.

Power Tools used:

Retrieval, Spacing, Interleaving, Metacognition

Examples of Pacing Guides (QR code supplied by Courtney Ostaff).

JUSTIN RIDENOUR

Grade level taught: 6th and 7th grades, ages 11–12

Subject: Science

years teaching: 9

School: Governor Thomas Johnson Middle School

District: Frederick County Public Schools

Location: Frederick, Maryland, USA

X (formerly Twitter): @RidenourEAATS

How did you become interested in the science of teaching and learning? Describe your path to evidence-informed teaching.

During the summer of 2020, I attended a virtual Mind Brain Education (MBE) summer deep-dive workshop that was conducted through The Center for Transformative Teaching and Learning (CTTL). During this workshop, I remember hearing Patrice Bain speak during her session about her story and the *Powerful Teaching*[16] tool. I found myself immediately purchasing the book and finished reading it before the next school year started. I was excited to learn about various and practical ways to support learning in the classroom by using these effective strategies. My excitement continued into the next school year when I was able to facilitate a book study using the *Powerful Teaching* book. During the fall 2020 session, I and five other educators read through the book and discussed how we see these strategies supporting students in our classrooms. My book, which is well-loved, has numerous pink tabs to track everything I was already doing or what I wanted to implement. That year, I jumped headfirst with using various Power Tools to support students' learning.

Strategy: Weekly Retrieval Grids

How do you use this strategy?

The most exciting strategy I took away from learning about Power Tools was the use of retrieval grids. Wednesdays became known as "Retrieval Wednesdays" as students had a grid each week. The retrieval grids were simple, yet effective, when it came to supporting students' "pulling out information." Each grid contains nine questions. Three of the questions were from current information, while the other six were from previous learning modules. Each weekly retrieval grid had the answers linked at the bottom of the page for students to access. The answers were linked to keep the grid low-stakes.

Power Tools used:

Retrieval, Spacing, Interleaving, Metacognition

Example of a Retrieval Grid Practice Challenge (QR code supplied by Justin Ridenour).

Retrieval Grid Practice Challenge! Respond on slide 2

1. From term 1: True/False: In order for kinetic energy to exist, potential energy must also exist.	2. From term 1: Which type of energy is stored energy? Kinetic or Potential	3. From term 1: Which products do living things make after breathing?	Way Back Learning
4. From term 2: Which living thing makes its own food? Consumer or Producer	5. From term 2: If an organism eats only plants it is called a _____ consumer.	6. From term 2: When two poles are similar such as, North and North or South and South. These poles would _____.	Last Term Learning
7. True/False: The seafloor is spreading due to magma pushing up through the crust.	8. Which boundary "divides" or moves away from each other?	9. Which boundary "collides" or moves toward each other?	Current Learning

Student Response Slide!

1.	2.	3.	Way Back Learning
4.	5.	6.	Last Term Learning
7.	8.	9.	Current Learning

Retrieval Grid Answer Slide-Link separately

1. True	2. Potential Energy	3. Carbon Dioxide	Way Back Learning
4. Producer	5. Primary Consumer	6. Repel (Push away from each other)	Last Term Learning
7. True	8. Divergent Boundary	9. Convergent Boundary	Current Learning

SHANE SAEED

District: St Vrain Valley School District

Location: Colorado, USA

X (formerly Twitter): @saeed_shane

How are evidence-informed teaching and learning used in your school and/or district?

In St Vrain Valley Schools (SVVSD) we have a large emphasis on evidence-based practices to guide instructional practices and curriculums. Over the past five years, we have trained hundreds of teachers in science of learning practices through our year-long professional learning collaboratives, school-based professional development, district conferences, and book studies on *Powerful Teaching*.[17] The teachers who have committed to using two to three practices consistently have seen student outcomes increase exponentially. Important discussions being had include an emphasis on learning and growth over being "correct" as well as understanding it is OK to engage in desirable difficulty because it is where we learn the most. Through our collaborative, teachers are taught to monitor data and use power standards to guide retrieval practice. They monitor how well retrieval is going in their classrooms and collaborate with other members to discuss how to overcome barriers to their practice and/or to enhance the practices that are working well. It's a community of learners where we continue to elevate and refine our practices.

How is the science of learning incorporated into professional development?

As a coach, I use science of learning practices in my coaching sessions with both teachers and administrators, as well as through my professional development sessions. In my work with teachers [I use science of learning] to tap into their metacognition in order to plan in terms of identifying success indicators and strategies they have successfully used before. With both teachers and administrators, I lean heavily on reflection to have the coachee think about how something went. The most powerful and long-term changes come from self-reflection and the coachee coming to their own conclusions. I provide feedback as necessary, but the majority of the cognitive processes are put on the teacher or administrator. During the professional development classes I facilitate I bring in retrieval practices to support information retention from our session together. I encourage teachers to use these practices to support their own professional learning, either through graduate programs, professional development sessions, or professional reading they do on their own.

ADELLE SAGER

Role: College Student

University: Western Washington University

Location: Bellingham, Washington, USA

How has learning about learning changed your study habits?

Learning about metacognition and understanding long-term versus short-term memory has helped me in all my classes with high volumes of memorization and content. Rather than rereading notes or looking at images of slides, I can use my active recall strategies for spaced study bursts. I talk to so many people in my classes who tell me that they don't know how to study or what their process should be. It is understandable that these techniques cannot be applied to every discipline or subject, but I argue that everyone should think about their habits and success stories with regards to a time where they excelled in a test or long-term memory development. Developing a passion for learning rather than earning a letter in a class is what really changed when I applied these techniques.

Strategy: Drawing-based Retrieval

How do you use this strategy?

I will draw an image of the body system or cell that I am studying and then start labeling the image with the information I remember about said image. I use this strategy to test my understanding of biology. I find it helps me compartmentalize the systems or processes of a larger system and forces me to have a continuous stream of information put out on the page. I will try to do this multiple times before the test. I use different colors to signify the material I need to review, or the material I forgot about. This is especially effective for biological sciences, or sciences of the body.

Power Tools used:

Retrieval, Spacing, Interleaving, Metacognition

Note from Patrice:

Adelle Sager is a college student and I am delighted to include her in this chapter.

I wanted to illustrate that when students are taught *how to learn*, they are able to independently bring forth and *use* the information stored in their memory. This wasn't "cramming the night before the exam," rather, it was weeks of spaced retrieval, interleaving, and testing metacognition for accuracy.

Thank you, Adelle Sager, for showing all of us the fruits of our labor when we teach students how to learn.

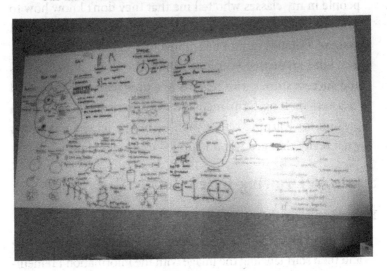

In the photo, Adelle found a large wall-sized whiteboard in an empty study room. Using Drawing-based Retrieval, she created this masterpiece retrieving everything she had learned about cells in a college course to help prepare herself for the exam.

In another example, Adelle started with a simple drawing of a human body.

She began with using the body illustration and breaking down her retrieval into categories.

Levels of organization:

- organism

- origins

- tissues

- cells
- chemicals
- endochondral bone formation
- bone growth and repair
- types of bones
- skin
- layers of epidermis, dermis
- organs
- internal vs. external cell environment

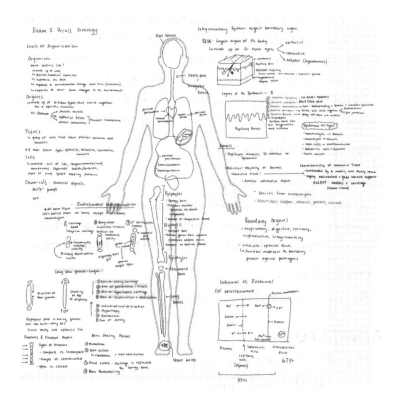

Although the image is difficult to read, I wanted you to see the process Adelle used in this Drawing-based Retrieval.[18]

KAREN SCHULTE

Grade level taught: 2nd grade, age 8

Subject: General Education

years teaching: 23

School: Legacy Elementary

District: St. Vrain Valley School District

Location: Longmont, Colorado, USA

How did you become interested in the science of teaching and learning? Describe your path to evidence-informed teaching.

Over the years I have noticed students remembering less as time went on. I would spend hours trying to make my lessons rigorous, engaging, fun, interactive, etc. Yet, a few months later, it was gone. I took a good look at me – *how* was I teaching? Maybe I need to tweak my practice? And then I was introduced to the Science of Learning Collaborative Professional Development.

Strategy: Brain Dump

How do you use this strategy?

At the start of a unit, I ask my students to write everything they know about the topic in one color. At the end of each lesson, they pick a different color and add the new information.

Power Tools used:

Retrieval, Spacing, Metacognition

ANNE STOKKE

Grade level taught: University

Subjects: Math and Statistics

University: University of Winnipeg

Location: Winnipeg, Manitoba, Canada

X (formerly Twitter): @rastokke

Strategy: A, B, C, D

How do you use this strategy?

In the fall term, I gave my entire class of 60 calculus students index cards labeled A, B, C, D and regularly asked retrieval practice questions and check-for-understanding questions throughout the class. It was probably one of the most effective and simple techniques I've implemented in 20 years of teaching – and it was your idea! Every student had to participate and pay attention and they were really engaged in the class. Profs normally use things like iClicker apps but this requires phones in class, something I don't allow, because students will get distracted with other things on their phones. Plus, the students felt some obligation to try to get the right answer because they knew I could see what they answered. So, I really want to thank you for this. I will be using this technique again this term!

Power Tools used:

Retrieval, Spacing, Metacognition

Note from Patrice:

I have also included Dr. Stokke in the Influencer section of this book. When I was a guest on her podcast, she told me about a strategy she often uses. I am including it here in this chapter.

ALISON STONE

Grade level taught: 10–12 grades, 16–18-year-olds

Subjects: Anatomy and Physiology

years teaching: 18

School: Central Bucks High School West

District: Central Bucks School District

Location: Pennsylvania, USA

X (formerly Twitter): @alisonstoneBIO

How did you become interested in the science of teaching and learning? Describe your path to evidence-informed teaching.

A colleague suggested I listen to the Cult of Pedagogy Podcast because I was struggling with my National Board Certification. I listened to six powerful learning strategies when Jennifer Gonzalez interviewed Megan Smith Sumeracki and Yana Weinstein. I was hooked. I went on to write two blogs for The Learning Scientists about my experience using retrieval and spaced practice in the classroom.

Strategy: List – Pass – Amass

How do you use this strategy?

Task 1: Each group (3–4 students) is assigned one topic/chapter. They use their notes to identify essential knowledge. They work together to draft open-ended questions which they write in chalk markers on the desks.

Task 2: All resources are put away; groups rotate to the next desk. They have five minutes to answer questions using retrieval. After five minutes [they] rotate to a new desk and repeat Task 2; continue.

Task 3: Students rotate one last time and this time they review the answers of the other groups. They identify further questions or clarifications which are discussed by the whole group.

Power Tools used:

Retrieval, Spacing, Metacognition

Strategy: Reflective Test Corrections

How do you use this strategy?

My Advanced Placement (AP) students use this activity because learning should not end with a unit assessment. The day after the exam, students receive a copy of the exam with each incorrect question circled. (The correct answer is not provided.) Students use the list on the "Why I Got This Question Incorrect" document to code their corrections. Students are allowed to use any handwritten notes during corrections but otherwise it is a testing environment.

Adapted from Daniel Willingham's *Outsmart Your Brain*.

Power Tools used:

Metacognition

Assessment Reflection

Name: _____   **Block:**

Title of Assessment:
Original Score Earned:

Question Number	My Answer	Why did you miss the question (code with number)?	Correct Answer (and explain why it is the correct choice)

GLENN WHITMAN

Grade level taught: 10th grade, age 15

Subject: History

years teaching: 31 (and going strong)

School: St. Andrew's Episcopal School

District: Montgomery County, Maryland

Location: Potomac, Maryland, USA

X (formerly Twitter)/LinkedIn: @gwhitmancttl, https://www.linkedin.com/in/gwhitman/

How did you become interested in the science of teaching and learning? Describe your path to evidence-informed teaching.

I am fortunate to be at a school that in 2007 asked itself the question, "How do you take good teachers and make them great and great teachers and make them expert?" Our answer was the Science of Teaching and Learning, or more specifically Mind, Brain, and Education (MBE) after connecting with Dr. Kurt Fischer and his team at Harvard's Graduate School of Education. This has led to a sustained yet iterative professional development focus on translating to our instructional design and work with all students the most promising research and strategies in the science of how the adult and student brain learns, works, and thrives. We avoided the "one-and-done" professional learning experience or "year of the brain" theme by establishing The Center for Transformative Teaching and Learning (www.thecttl.org) that continues to guide this work for our teachers, students, families, and educators around the world.

Strategy: Weekly Retrieval Grid Formative Assessments

How do you use this strategy?

Weekly teacher- and student-designed retrieval grid formative assessments, inspired by Pooja Agarwal and Retrieval Practice, challenge students to think hard and retrieve from their long-term memory historical content and skills presented last class, last week, and even last month. These low- or no-stakes assessments provide the teacher and each student [with] immediate evidence that can inform what might need to be taught again or evidence of student readiness to build upon this "secured" knowledge and historical methods skills.

Power Tools used:

Retrieval, Spacing, Metacognition

Note from Patrice:

You will also find The Center for Transformative Teaching and Learning listed in the Resources section.

Look at an example of a Retrieval Grid that Glenn uses.

War, Government, and Research Retrieval Grid

What battle launched the American Revolutionary War with the "short heard around the world?"	America's "first Constitution" was called what?	Wikipedia and Britannica would all be considered what type of research source?
Which battle is considered the turning point of the Revolutionary War as it led to France's support of the colonists' war effort?	Name **ONE** way in which America's "1" Constitution was a product of the colonies, relationship with England?	What **three** Terms of the Historian have been most relevant to the early stages of the Scholarly Research Paper Project?
After what battle in Virginia did General Cornwallis surrender to George Washington?	Who said the following: "The real revolution was not the war but the system of government that came out of it"?	What is **ONE**, indisputable fact about your research paper topic?
Complete the Chain of Historical Causation		Complete the Chain of Historical Causation

Thomas Paine's *Common Sense* (January 1776)

Salutary Neglect 1698–1754 → French-Indian War 1754–1763 → Taxes $ + Troops (¾ Acts) Stamp Tax Townshend Duties → Declaration of Independence

Battle of Lexington and Concord (1775) "Shot Heard Around the World"

American Revolutionary War 1775–1783

1787/1788

1741

CAROL WOODS

Grade level taught: Preschool, ages 3–5

Subjects: Literacy, Math, Writing, Science

years teaching: 13

School: Red Hawk Elementary

District: St. Vrain Valley School District

Location: Erie, Colorado, USA

How did you become interested in the science of teaching and learning? Describe your path to evidence-informed teaching.

I took the *Powerful Teaching*[19] Book Study through our district's Professional Development. I was particularly curious about retrieval practices. I then joined our district's Science of Learning Collaborative to learn from other teachers the strategies they use in their classrooms to help students retrieve information. I began using the strategies in my classroom to help students with their number recognition, their letter/sound knowledge, and to build their metacognition. I wanted to see if these strategies would work in preschool and they do!

Strategies: Retrieval Practice, Fishbowl, Turn and Talk, Thinking Maps, Think-Pair-Share, and Retrieve Letters

How do you use these strategies?

I use several different strategies. I first began with **thinking maps**. I use the maps to retrieve information we have read from a book or different words that begin with the letters of the alphabet. We use **turn and talk** to retrieve facts from books such as: *What Do Bears Eat?* The students then do a turn and talk about all the things a bear eats and then they share out. We use the **fishbowl** for letters, letter sounds, numbers, and sight words that have been introduced to see what the students are retrieving. We use **think-pair-share** to discuss our question of the day such as: Why do bears live in caves or dens? The students write a letter on the whiteboard that was learned a couple days ago, point to their brains, and say retrieve letter A and then write letter A.

Power Tools used:

Retrieval, Spacing, Metacognition

Look at the pictures of Carol's strategies.

Letter Retrieval

Fishbowl Letters

Thinking Map: Double Bubble Compare and Contrast Bears

NOTES

1. Galea, Erika. (2024). Understanding how we think: Why educators need to know how the brain learns. *The Sunday Times of Malta*, 24th March. Available at https://timesofmalta.com/article/understanding-think.1089521 [Accessed 24 March 2024].

2. One-pager format credit to https://nowsparkcreativity.com/.

3. Further details can be found at https://docs.google.com/presentation/d/e/2PACX-1vRcTA1x8T7QWROGut0DA5qVD BiX0n_WqoBg0sB_8f31yPunCsvCUMTDvU2apowSXTcTof 5HkzMA1kI/pub?start=false&loop=false&delayms=3000&slide =id.p.

4. Whitman, Glenn, and Ian Kelleher. *Neuroteach: Brain Science and the Future of Education.* Lanham, MD: Rowman and Littlefield, 2016.

5. Brown, Peter C., Henry L. Roediger, and Mark A. McDaniel. *Make It Stick: The Science of Successful Learning.* Cambridge, MA: Harvard University Press, 2014.

6. Agarwal, Pooja K., and Patrice M. Bain. *Powerful Teaching: Unleash the Science of Learning.* San Francisco: Jossey-Bass, 2019.

7. Further details can be found at https://docs.google.com/ document/d/1AyKuTrQ0OHILtQPdhkcFBpDp3MuB12jTQbL qp7tZwzU/edit.

8. Further details can be found at https://drive.google.com/file/ d/19wt-gMY-sGqAvNldsOrIJZnv8zM4kjbb/view.

9. Further details can be found at https://theeffortfuleducator .com/2019/03/13/brain-book-buddy-a-strategy-for-ssessment/.

10. Further details can be found at https://theeffortfuleducator .com/wp-content/uploads/2020/06/Brain-Book-Buddy-1-3.pdf.

11. Agarwal, Pooja K., and Patrice M. Bain. *Powerful Teaching: Unleash the Science of Learning.* San Francisco: Jossey-Bass, 2019.

12. Agarwal, Pooja K., and Patrice M. Bain. *Powerful Teaching: Unleash the Science of Learning.* San Francisco: Jossey-Bass, 2019.

13. Agarwal, Pooja K., and Patrice M. Bain. *Powerful Teaching: Unleash the Science of Learning.* San Francisco: Jossey-Bass, 2019.

14. Jones, Kate. *Retrieval Practice.* Woodbridge: John Catt Publishing, 2019.

15. Agarwal, Pooja K., and Patrice M. Bain. *Powerful Teaching: Unleash the Science of Learning.* San Francisco: Jossey-Bass, 2019.

16. Agarwal, Pooja K., and Patrice M. Bain. *Powerful Teaching: Unleash the Science of Learning.* San Francisco: Jossey-Bass, 2019.

17. Agarwal, Pooja K., and Patrice M. Bain. *Powerful Teaching: Unleash the Science of Learning.* San Francisco: Jossey-Bass, 2019.

18. Please request the image from https://drive.google.com/ open?id=1qjzYWB1RS1wtOHdUnzEW_YSvzXV-ABlT&usp= drive_copy.

19. Agarwal, Pooja K., and Patrice M. Bain. *Powerful Teaching: Unleash the Science of Learning.* San Francisco: Jossey-Bass, 2019.

Chapter 8

Influencers

What really knocks me out is a book that, when you're all done reading it, you wish the author that wrote it was a terrific friend of yours and you could call him up on the phone whenever you felt like it.

J.D. Salinger

To paraphrase Salinger's quote:

What really knocks me out is an article, podcast, book that, when you're all done listening or reading it, you wish the author who wrote it was a terrific friend of yours . . . and you could contact that person and they agreed to be in your own book.

Because this is exactly what happened and I feel like the most fortunate person on the planet.

Each person in the following chapter is someone who influenced me through their writing or conversations. I am humbled and honored to be forever "linked in ink" with my edu-heroes. Each person was asked the same three questions:

- Of your own books, articles, blogs, and/or podcasts, which is your favorite and why?
- Thinking of others' books, articles, blogs, and/or podcasts, what are your top three to recommend to others?
- Thinking about the science of learning, who influences you?

We are fortunate to have access to evidence-informed information readily available. A caveat, however, is making sure the evidence is real and tested; as information becomes widespread, so do false claims. Whom can we trust? How can we ensure our precious time is not wasted falling down rabbit holes or spending money on false claims? The following people are those whom I trust. They are generous with their resources and can easily be followed on social media.

I encourage you to continue on your science of learning path and please join me by making use of their wisdom.

POOJA AGARWAL, Ph.D.

Role: Associate Professor of Psychology

Organization: Berklee College of Music

Location: Boston, Massachusetts, USA

X (formerly Twitter): @RetrieveLearn, @PoojaAgarwal

Of your own books, articles, blogs, and/or podcasts, which is your favorite and why?

Of my work, I am proudest of the book *Powerful Teaching*, my keynote for SXSW EDU in 2022, my literature review of 50 experiments on retrieval practice conducted in classroom settings (Agarwal, Nunes, and Blunt, 2021), and my 100+ free resources at retrievalpractice.org. The evolution of these works has been deeply rewarding to envision, create, and share, originating from my initial research in college and now reaching an international audience of educators and schools. Each book, video, and article, in its own way, highlights the rigor of cognitive science research while also making research-based teaching strategies accessible and practical – a balance that has taken me decades to find. I continue to be inspired by my students and I am grateful for educators from around the world who are transforming teaching and learning.

- Subscribe for Dr. Agarwal's newsletter:
  - https://www.retrievalpractice.org/subscribe
- News interviews with Vox and ASCD:
  - https://www.vox.com/even-better/23785695/learn-something-new-every-day-retrieval-practice
  - https://www.ascd.org/blogs/retrieval-practice-one-minute-to-better-student-learning
- Podcast interviews with NPR and Cult of Pedagogy:
  - https://www.npr.org/2019/09/03/757161013/how-to-do-well-and-be-happy-in-college
  - https://www.cultofpedagogy.com/retrieval-practice/
- Dr. Agarwal's keynote at SXSW EDU on YouTube:
  - https://www.youtube.com/watch?v=OUl0mMVbkAc&t=331s
- Recommended research publication (Agarwal, Nunes, and Blunt, 2021, *Educational Psychology Review*)
  - https://rdcu.be/cgite
- *Powerful Teaching* on Amazon:
  - https://www.amazon.com/gp/product/111952184X/ref=as_li_ss_tl?ie=UTF8&linkCode=sl1&tag=retrievalprac-20&linkId=f0c7d8f24f4622ccebfae32d00dec1eb&language=en_US

Thinking about the science of learning, who influences you?

I am heavily influenced and inspired by my colleagues listed at retrievalpractice.org/scientists. If I had to pick resources from others, I recommend all the work by my colleagues, especially **The Learning Scientists**.

> **Patrice's note:** The stars aligned in August 2005, when Pooja Agarwal, cognitive scientist from Washington University in St. Louis, Missouri, met me at the staircase of Columbia Middle School in Columbia, Illinois. From the moment we met, we had an intuitive understanding of what works in a classroom. The rest, they say, is history. We helped devise the research that occurred in my classroom. We thought, we constructed, we tweaked and what emerged has become a gold standard for the possibilities of learning for students. Dr. Agarwal conducted the research needed for her dissertation in my classroom. I have learned so much, and continue to learn, from Dr. Agarwal. She has incredible knowledge and is a champion for women scientists. Dr. Agarwal shares research with over 20,000 teachers weekly. She regularly posts to our *Powerful Teaching* Book Club, www.facebook.com/groups/powerfulteaching, which has thousands of members. Her Practice Guides, on so many learning topics and in different languages, are only a download away (www.retrievalpractice.org). She has widened my horizons and most importantly, to me, has become a dear and lifelong friend.

SILVIA BASTOW

Role: Head of Languages

Location: Widnes, Cheshire, UK

X (formerly Twitter): https://twitter.com/SisaSilvia4

Of your own books, articles, blogs, and/or podcasts, which is your favorite and why?

Effective strategies to support novice and expert learners – "The Power of Modelling" – an article for the *Chartered College of Teaching Impact Journal.*

In a subject like MFL [Modern Foreign Languages], which requires output based on a cumulative build-up of knowledge, the importance of modelling examples of excellence in languages classrooms, via teacher or expert learners, cannot be underestimated.

It is always an honor to write for such a prestigious educational journal based on research and evidence-based practice.

Thinking of others' books, articles, blogs, and/or podcasts, what are your top three to recommend to others?

- https://podcasts.apple.com/gb/podcast/the-motivated-classroom/id1525120086 – excellent for world languages teachers
- *Memory* by S. Smith and G. Conti – cognitive science and Second Language Acquisition (SLA)
- *Making Every MFL Lesson Count* – James A. Maxwell

Thinking about the science of learning, who influences you?

- Chartered College of Teaching (https://chartered.college/aboutus/) – as they are research-informed and provide examples from actual classrooms.
- Association for Language Learning (https://www.all-languages.org.uk/) – as they provide evidence-based strategies for SLA and a lot of CPD, often free for Languages teachers.
- *Powerful Teaching* by Pooja Agarwal and Patrice Bain – I really enjoyed your book.
- *Retrieval Practice* series by Kate Jones (John Catt Publishing).

- *WalkThrus* by Tom Sherrington and Oliver Caviglioli (John Catt Publishing).

- Various colleagues on X – **Tom Sherrington** (https://twitter.com/teacherhead), **Michael Chiles** (https://twitter.com/m_chiles), **Kate Jones**, and **Haili Hughes**.

Patrice's note: I had the pleasure of meeting Silvia when we were co-presenters for a Seneca webinar. Her ideas resonated with me and I have been a follower ever since. Her knowledge of languages, and how to teach them, is unparalleled.

FLAVIA BELHAM, Ph.D.

Location: London, UK

X (formerly Twitter)/LinkedIn: @flaviabelhamphd, https://www.linkedin.com/in/flaviasbelham/

Of your own books, articles, blogs, and/or podcasts, which is your favorite and why?

My favourite work so far has been a series of webinars that I organised and hosted during the pandemic. They were all about the science of learning, featuring academics, researchers, teachers and writers of all subjects and from multiple countries. Some of them had over 1,000 attendees watching it live and thousands of other views on the YouTube videos. COVID-19 was a hard time for schools and teachers, who had to suddenly reorganise and rethink almost everything they were doing. So being able to bring so many people together (even if virtually) to discuss the science of learning was really special. You can find the videos here: https://www.youtube.com/@SenecaCPD/playlists.

Thinking of others' books, articles, blogs, and/or podcasts, what are your top three to recommend to others?

- The blog by Blake Harvard. He shares incredible posts about the science of learning with actual examples of activities he uses in his classroom (https://theeffortfuleducator.com/).

- The book *Dual Coding with Teachers* by Oliver Caviglioli. Very easy to follow with great practical examples.
- The book series *Retrieval Practice* by Kate Jones. Filled with evidence-informed discussions and practical ideas to apply in the classroom.

Thinking about the science of learning, who influences you?

The Learning Scientists do an amazing job bridging academic work with real-life school applications. Having come from a research background, I have always thought most academic papers on the science of learning were too theoretical and did not really offer anything tangible for school teachers to use with their students. But when I came across Megan Sumeracki, Carolina Kuepper-Tetzel and their colleagues' work I realised that it was possible to bring scientific research into the classroom and have a direct positive impact on learning.

> **Patrice's note:** I had the pleasure of meeting Dr. Belham through the Seneca Tutoring Webinars. She invited me to be a guest in 2022. Here is the webinar "Parents: Learn how to help your children to study more effectively!" (https://www.youtube.com/watch?v=aDs5dXASc6Q&t=233s). Be sure to check out her YouTube link to find a wealth of webinars!

NATHAN BURNS

Location: UK

X (formerly Twitter): @MrMetacognition

Of your own books, articles, blogs, and/or podcasts, which is your favorite and why?

Favourite published work: with all of my published work, I have focused on accessibility and practicality. If time-short educators are taking the time to engage with my work, then they need something actionable to come out of it! We don't have the time to be reading swathes of theory with no real strategies to put into place. I know that Patrice shares these aims. Considering this, I'm extremely proud of my first book, *Inspiring Deep Learning with Metacognition: A Guide for Secondary Teaching*, which provides copious strategies that are ready to instantly introduce into the classroom. Though extremely useful, I wonder whether my more recent project, *Teaching Hacks: Fixing Everyday Classroom Issues with Metacognition* may be even more helpful? This book focuses on perennial classroom issues – improved verbal student responses, quality of reading, revision techniques, and so forth, and provides proven metacognitive approaches to help tackle them. I really hope that this book provides the strategies that teachers, UK and worldwide, need to improve their teaching and student outcomes.

Thinking of others' books, articles, blogs, and/or podcasts, what are your top three to recommend to others?

- Top recommendations: being UK-based, and a research nerd, my go-to for research has (and probably always will be!) the EEF – the Education Endowment Foundation (https://educationendowmentfoundation.org.uk/).

- Having spent so much time focused on metacognition in my work, I have used their guide on metacognition so many times (https://educationendowmentfoundation.org.uk/ education-evidence/guidance-reports/metacognition). It is a practical and easy to read document.

- My second top read would be *Strengthening the Student Toolbox* by John Dunlosky. It covers the range of revision strategies, and which are more effective than others. Another easy and actionable read (https://files.eric .ed.gov/fulltext/EJ1021069.pdf).

- Finally, I'm a big fan of Craig Barton. He has focused more on the Maths side of things, but has covered some very interesting approaches, including variation theory. His book, *Reflect, Expect, Check, Explain: Sequences and Behaviour to Enable Mathematical Thinking in the Classroom*, is a great read.

Thinking about the science of learning, who influences you?

As a researcher and practitioner, I'm very solution-focused, placing great emphasis on efficiency. I find that one author who really chimes with me is **Daniel T. Willingham**. Daniel's work is very solution-focused, breaking problems down nicely, getting to the nub of the problem, and providing solutions to some crucial issues in education.

> **Patrice's note:** I began following Nathan Burns on X (formerly Twitter); with a name such as "Mr. Metacognition," how could I resist? I am quite honored to have written a chapter in his book *Teaching Hacks: Fixing Everyday Classroom Issues with Metacognition*. Nathan's books are a great addition to your library.

BRADLEY BUSCH

Location: London, UK

X (formerly Twitter): @BradleyKBusch

Of your own books, articles, blogs, and/or podcasts, which is your favorite and why?

I loved writing our book, *The Science of Learning*, as I just felt that exploring research, that is behind paywalls and is often quite inaccessible, was exciting as there is a treasure trove of information and guidance that exists out there. As such, being able to bring those research papers to a mainstream audience felt brilliant. That being said, our most recent book, *Teaching and Learning Illuminated*, was really fun to write as we enjoyed the challenge of taking complex research and representing it in a beautiful visual format.

Thinking of others' books, articles, blogs, and/or podcasts, what are your top three to recommend to others?

- There is a wealth of amazing books, blogs and podcasts that exist out there. My favourite book that I have ever read in education is called *Cleverlands* by an educator called Lucy Crehan. It is exceptional. She details her experience of teaching in a range of countries and what we can learn from these different settings.
- My favourite article is one by Dr. Zach Groshell (https://educationrickshaw.com/2021/12/01/how-cognitive-load-theory-changed-my-teaching/). I love how he draws on research and is honest with his self-reflections.
- The podcast I listen to the most is TandTeaching (https://podcasts.apple.com/us/podcast/tandteaching-the-educational-podcast). I learn so much.

Thinking about the science of learning, who influences you?
There are many science of learning giants on whose shoulders we are all standing. I think the unsung heroes out there are the researchers who painstakingly and methodically run experiments that give us insight into how learning happens. Often, they don't seek the limelight and may not be well known, but their work forms the basis of everything we know.

Patrice's note: I began following Bradley Busch years ago on X (formerly Twitter). I thought his writings often hit the targets I was seeking. Brad contacted me about writing an article which led to an actual phone conversation! We decided the article should be titled "In the Room Where It Happened" and I have used the phrase many times since. Here is a link to the article: https://www.innerdrive.co.uk/

blog/cognitive-science-origins/. I was delighted to meet Brad in person, attend his presentation, and enjoy his camaraderie at the Festival of Education in Maryland in 2023. I encourage you to follow Brad on social media and sign up for his webinars. His work with InnerDrive (https://www.innerdrive.co.uk/education-resources/) should be in everyone's professional development toolbox.

OLIVER CAVIGLIOLI

Location: Essex, UK

X (formerly Twitter): @olicav

Of your own books, articles, blogs, and/or podcasts, which is your favorite and why?

Dual Coding with Teachers: It's captured all of the various elements in one place and shows how to develop your practice in each.
Teaching WalkThrus: my collaboration with Tom Sherrington, for me, represented the power of the above-mentioned *Dual Coding* applied to teacher professional development.

Thinking of others' books, articles, blogs, and/or podcasts, what are your top three to recommend to others?

- *Napkin Sketch Workbook* by Don Moyer is the best on verbal communication and terse text
- James Britton's 1970 *Language and Learning*
- *Graphics for Learning* by Ruth Clark and Chopeta Lyons

Thinking about the science of learning, who influences you?

Paul Kirschner and **Logan Fiorella**

Patrice's note: I had been following Oliver Caviglioli for several years and was always impressed with his drawings; they conveyed simplicity yet told a story without ever needing words. I have a UK version of *WalkThrus*, which has since become a widely popular series. I admired what I thought of as a select club, those people who were fortunate to have a Caviglioli portrait. When the US version of *WalkThrus* was being developed, I was asked to conduct a prepublish read. And with that, I was able to join others with my very own Caviglioli portrait! I was able to meet Oliver at the Festival of Education in Maryland in 2023. I was lucky to have a couple between-events strolls with him. No wonder he is such a talented artist; he has a very keen eye for design.

TONI ROSE DEANON

Role: Community Engagement

Location: Montgomery, Alabama, USA

X (formerly Twitter)/LinkedIn: @classroomflex, linkedin.com/in/tonirosedeanon/

Of your own books, articles, blogs, and/or podcasts, which is your favorite and why?

The article published in Edutopia "Teaching Revision in a Blended Learning Environment" (https://www.edutopia.org/article/teaching-revision-blended-learning-environment/) is hands down my favorite because I got to co-write it with one of my teacher-besties, Emily Culp, and we were so excited to show how we created time for revisions in our English classrooms, a challenge that many educators face. There is so much pride in being able to share what we did in our own classrooms, in hopes that it will help educators who read our article.

Thinking of others' books, articles, blogs, and/or podcasts, what are your top three to recommend to others?

- *Coaching for Equity* by Elana Aguilar
- Modern Classrooms Project Podcast, https://podcast.modernclassrooms.org/
- *Start Here, Start Now* by Liz Kleinrock

Thinking about the science of learning, who influences you?

Dr. Pooja Agarwal is the one who put me on the science of learning with retrieval practice and I continue to share her strategies and research with educators I work with. I make sure to implement what I learn in the professional development sessions I lead for educators all over the world.

Patrice's note: I first met Toni Rose when I was contacted to do a webinar for the Modern Classroom Project. It was a delight to work with her and Alison Stone on this project. (Find Alison Stone in the Teachers and Leaders in Chapter 7.) The link for the Modern Classroom Project is rich with information! Here is the link for my webinar:

Modern Classroom Project with Patrice Bain, Toni Rose Deanon, and Alison Stone: https://www.modernclassrooms.org/calendar/retrieval-practice-other-powerful-teaching-techniques

Here is a link to a talk Toni Rose had with Dr. Agarwal:

Modern Classroom Project with Dr. Pooja Agarwal and Toni Rose Deanon: https://podcast.modernclassrooms.org/115

KENNET FRÖJD

Roles: Author, Podcaster, Inclusion Specialist, Principal at Celsius School

Location: Edsbyn, Sweden

Fröjd's Toolbox (Spotify, Amazon, Podbean): www.frojdstool box.se

X (formerly Twitter): @frojds_toolbox

Of your own books, articles, blogs, and/or podcasts, which is your favorite and why?

My podcast "Fröjd's Toolbox" where I interview top-class experts on evidence-informed learning, teaching, and leading.

I am like a kid at Christmas at every interview. I learn so much by myself. But my aim is that the listeners will learn more, even if they have already read all the work of my guests. The podcast started with a focus on a Swedish audience, but more than half of the guests are international experts. After receiving a number of requests, all international episodes (in English) are promoted via X to make them accessible for a global audience. A few years ago, I had a book idea based on feedback I received from many teachers. The idea was how to organize the book and make it inclusive and useful for every teacher/reader. I approached two international experts with different backgrounds that both had greatly impressed me. Both of them agreed to do this with me. The two are Wendy Murawski (Professor of Special Education) and Jennifer Austin (Professor of Psychology). Together, we developed the concept for the book, based on evidence-informed strategies, and during that process we realized more and more how complementary we were to each other. Initially, we simply called the book "The Unique Book Project" until it got an official title. I am very proud of the resulting book that in 2024 was published in an English version – *Practical Strategies for Managing a Diverse Classroom, K-6: The Teacher's Toolkit* (Murawski, Fröjd's, and Austin, 2024).

Thinking of others' books, articles, blogs, and/or podcasts, who influences you and what are your top three to recommend to others?

This is very difficult to say because I am strongly inspired by many amazing experts around the world. It is very difficult to just mention three. It would have been easier if it was limited to 30! Below I will highlight three of my favorites that mean a lot to me and that I think are valuable for every teacher and school leader.

- The Google site by Efrat Furst is excellent: https://sites .google.com/view/efratfurst/learning-in-the-brain. She is my favorite "science of learning/how we teach in classrooms" communicator. I also like how, in all of her communication, [she] applies what she is writing about. She has a unique skill in creating visuals that support what she is communicating, whether it be orally or in text.

- I think it is very important with classroom research, even though it is very complex and challenging, to draw conclusions. It is of great importance to get as close to reality as possible. The next step is trying to translate the research results into useful teaching practice. I have an excellent example of when that is done in a way that I think is very useful for teachers and easy for them to translate into their own classrooms. That is the book *Powerful Teaching: Unleash the Science of Learning* (Agarwal and Bain, 2019).

- Finally, I select another book that I also find very interesting and think contributes a very nice way of highlighting the science of learning. Actually, I selected two books together as my choice due to the importance of linking the science of learning with teaching strategies in the classroom. These books are *How Learning Happens: Seminal Works in Educational Psychology and What They Mean in Practice* (Kirschner and Hendrick, 2020) and *How Teaching Happens: Seminal Works in Teaching and Teacher Effectiveness and What They Mean to Practice* (Kirschner, Hendrick, and Heal, 2022).

Patrice's note: It is always an honor to be asked to be a guest on a podcast. Here is my episode with Kennet on Fröjd's Toolbox: https://open.spotify.com/episode/10P5xg JD3VezDLVtyyYvC0.

DR. ERIKA GALEA

Location: Malta, Europe

LinkedIn: https://www.linkedin.com/in/erika-galea/

Of your own books, articles, blogs, and/or podcasts, which is your favorite and why?

The Educational Neuroscience Hub blog is among my favourite creations because it serves as a dynamic platform where I present the latest findings and discussions in educational neuroscience. A variety of content formats, including blog posts, video blogs, and webinars, are adopted to appeal to a diverse range of audiences. This blog was created to bridge the gap between complex scientific research and practical classroom application, thereby making it accessible to educators, parents, and students alike. The blog features articles, insights, and resources that translate neuroscience research into understandable and actionable content for educational professionals. If you wish to delve further into the science of teaching and learning, click on the following link: https://educationalneurosciencehub.com/.

The book I've authored, *Generation Alpha*, published by a prestigious UK publisher, Oxford University Press, is another cherished work. It offers a comprehensive exploration of the behavioural changes in today's teenagers, delving into the neuroscience behind these shifts. The book focuses on how these changes impact teenagers' learning and behaviour, and provides educators with practical strategies and techniques to adapt their teaching methods accordingly. It aims to effectively prepare educators with theoretical knowledge and practical tools, enhancing the teaching learning process with robust scientific evidence.

Thinking of others' books, articles, blogs, and/or podcasts, what are your top three to recommend to others?

- The book that has profoundly inspired my passion for the science of teaching and learning is Dr. David Sousa's *How the Brain Learns*. This international bestseller, now in its sixth edition, is a testament to the evolving field of educational neuroscience. Dr. Sousa skillfully translates the latest brain research into practical strategies for the classroom, making it a game-changer for educators aiming to deliver brain-changing results. *How the Brain Learns* is not just a resource for enthusiasts of brain-compatible learning; it's a comprehensive guide that *fires educators' neurons*, equipping them with innovative tools to foster student success.

- *Educational Neuroscience: The Basics* is another book that has captured my attention with its comprehensive introduction to the field. Authored by Cathy Rogers and Michael S. C. Thomas, it blends educational neuroscience with human and social psychology, along with teacher expertise, to enhance student outcomes. The book delves into how the brain processes senses, emotions, and social interactions, and explores the complex mechanisms of thinking, learning, and memory. It offers practical classroom strategies, addresses special education needs, neurodiversity, and debunks neuromyths. This concise and engaging text is invaluable for students and professionals in psychology, neuroscience, and education, providing deep insights into the science of learning.

- *Powerful Teaching: Unleash the Science of Learning* is an essential read for educators seeking to enhance classroom effectiveness through cognitive science. Authored by cognitive scientist Pooja K. Agarwal, Ph.D., and experienced teacher Patrice M. Bain, Ed.S., this book translates complex research into practical classroom strategies. It highlights four key techniques: retrieval practice, spacing, interleaving, and feedback-driven metacognition. These methods are not only easy to implement but also significantly boost student achievement across various grades and subjects. The book draws from a rich pool of over 100 years of learning research and a 15-year collaboration between scientists and teachers. It serves as a valuable resource for educators aiming to elevate their teaching methods and foster deeper learning and knowledge retention in students.

Thinking about the science of learning, who influences you?

Dr. David A. Sousa, Ed.D., is an international consultant in educational neuroscience and author of 16 books that suggest ways that educators and parents can translate current brain research into strategies for improving learning. Dr. Sousa is an esteemed educational neuroscientist whose work has significantly influenced my perspective on teaching and learning. His pioneering efforts in bridging the gap between neuroscience and education, particularly through his practical applications of brain research in classroom settings, are both innovative and transformative. Dr. Sousa's insights into how children learn, and his strategies for enhancing the learning process, have reshaped my approach to education. His ability to translate complex neurological concepts into understandable and actionable teaching strategies is truly inspiring. His dedication to making neuroscience accessible and applicable to educators has not only deepened my understanding of how students learn but also empowered me to create more effective, engaging, and evidence-based learning environments. Dr. Sousa's work exemplifies the profound impact that understanding the human brain can have on educational practices, making him a source of inspiration and a guiding light in my educational journey.

Professor Andrew K. Tolmie, my former primary doctoral supervisor and a renowned developmental psychologist, has had a significant influence on me, inspires me profoundly for a multitude of reasons, and has been pivotal in shaping my academic journey. His exceptional expertise in the field of educational, developmental, and cognitive psychology, combined with a deep passion for academic research, sets a standard of excellence that I continually aspire to. What truly sets him apart, though, is his unparalleled mentorship style. He possesses a unique ability to challenge and stimulate intellectual curiosity while providing steadfast support and guidance. His insightful feedback and constructive criticism have not only sharpened my research skills but also instilled a robust confidence in my academic pursuits. Professor Tolmie's dedication to nurturing the potential in each of his students is evident in his patient and personalised approach to supervision. He encourages independent thinking and fosters an environment where questioning and exploration are not just allowed but actively encouraged. His commitment to academic integrity and ethical research practices also serves as a guiding beacon. Moreover, his professional accomplishments and contributions to the field are a constant source of inspiration, motivating me to strive for impact and excellence in my own career. The lessons learned under his tutelage extend beyond academia; they have been instrumental in shaping my personal growth and professional ethos.

Patrice's note: The Educational Neuroscience Hub (Dr. Galea mentioned above and provided the link) is a treasure of information. Whether seeking out individual topics or using it for a year's worth of professional development, I encourage you to check out this site. You will also find several of Galea's quotes in this book.

My introduction to and meeting with Dr. Galea on social media began over a mutual love of Malta, as I had visited several years prior and the country immediately became a favorite of mine. I was honored to be her guest and here is the link to both parts of our talk.

Part 1: https://educationalneurosciencehub.com/2023/07/
09/we-as-teachers-are-taught-how-to-teach-but-it-
is-really-rare-that-we-learn-how-our-students-learn-
delving-into-the-science-of-learning-patrice-bain/

Part 2: https://educationalneurosciencehub.com/2023/07/
23/too-often-we-as-teachers-do-not-give-the-students-
the-tools-to-discriminate-what-they-know-from-what-
they-dont-know-simply-by-learning-how-to-learn-and-
teaching-our-students-th/

ZACH GROSHELL

Roles: Instructional Coach, Teacher, Consultant

Location: Tacoma, Washington, USA

X (formerly Twitter): @mrzachg

Of your own books, articles, blogs, and/or podcasts, which is your favorite and why?

I host a podcast called "Progressively Incorrect" (https://
educationrickshaw.com/category/progressively-incorrect/). It
started out as a debate show between two teachers with very
different approaches to teaching, and now it has expanded to
interviews with some of the most important voices in education. Choosing my favorite is like choosing between my own
children, but check out my interview with Patrice Bain (of
course!), along with the interviews of Dan Willingham, Paul
Kirschner, Marcy Stein, and Pamela Snow. I also write blogs
for my website, educationrickshaw.com. My most popular
post is, "How Cognitive Load Theory Changed My Teaching"
(https://educationrickshaw.com/2021/12/01/how-cognitive-
load-theory-changed-my-teaching/comment-page-1/).

Thinking of others' books, articles, blogs, and/or podcasts, what are your top three to recommend to others?

I am a huge fan of the Education Research Reading Room
(ERRR) and Mr. Barton's Math Podcast. I recently joined

forces with these two lads to put together a crossover episode of all of our podcasts in this episode: https://educationrick shaw.com/2023/12/13/s3e3-craig-barton-and-ollie-lovell-on-tools-and-tips-for-teachers/).

I also recommend the book, *Explicit Instruction*, by Anita Archer and Charles Hughes. This book has helped me to refine my teaching so that it is clear, systematic, and meets the needs of my most vulnerable learners.

In addition, I recommend Anna Stokke's podcast, "Chalk and Talk," which explores the contentious debates around the "Math Wars." You can find my interview with Anna here: (https://educationrickshaw.com/2023/06/29/maximizing-learning-through-explicit-instruction-with-zach-groshell/).

Thinking about the science of learning, who influences you?

I am forever indebted to **Paul Kirschner**, **John Sweller**, and **Dick Clark** for their seminal work, "Why minimal guidance during instruction does not work: An analysis of the failure of constructivist, discovery, problem-based, experiential, and inquiry-based teaching," and the subsequent debates that it provoked, such as those documented in the book, *Constructivist Teaching: Success or Failure*. These debates were the inspiration for my podcast, "Progressively Incorrect." I am also a huge fan of the work of **Shana Carpenter**, **John Dunlosky**, **Ouhao Chen**, **Janet Metcalf**, **Richard Mayer**, and **Sigfried Englemann**.

> **Patrice's note:** The first time I met Zach was at the Festival of Education, Potomac, Maryland, in 2023. These conferences, along with researchEDs, are not only incredibly informative, they also bring together like-minded folks who are inspiring and provide a camaraderie of fun and good cheer. Zach fits that description. Later in 2023, I was a guest on his podcast "Progressively Incorrect: In the Room Where It Happened," and it has become one of my favorites. Here is the link: https://podcasts.apple.com/us/podcast/s3e4-patrice-bain-on-the-room-where-it-happened/

id1602317019?i=1000639284033. At researchED Greenwich (Connecticut, USA) Zach moderated a panel with
Tom Sherrington, Pedro De Bruyckere, and me.

Several of the people I am highlighting in this book have also
been on Zach's podcast. Here they are. Enjoy!

- Nidhi Sachdeva: (https://educationrickshaw.com/2023/03/15/
s2e24-nidhi-sachdeva-on-microlearning-and-cognitive-
science-principles/)

- Tom Sherrington and Oliver Caviglioli: (https://education
rickshaw.com/?s=tom+sherrington)

- Dan Willingham: (https://educationrickshaw.com/?s=dan
+willingham)

BLAKE HARVARD

Role: Teacher

Organization: James Clemens High School

Location: Madison, Alabama, USA

X (formerly Twitter): @effortfuleduktr

**Of your own books, articles, blogs, and/or podcasts, which is
your favorite and why?**

"Choke Points and Pitfalls in Studying" (https://theeffor
tfuleducator.com/2022/01/27/choke-points-and-pitfalls/). I
love this post because it is based in research and it is so easily accessible and applicable to a wide range of teachers and
students for positively shaping their understanding of memory and what sorts of barriers can get in the way of learning.

**Thinking of others' books, articles, blogs, and/or podcasts,
what are your top three to recommend to others?**

- *Powerful Teaching* by Pooja Agarwal, and Patrice Bain
- *Understanding How We Learn: A Visual Guide* by Yana
Weinstein, Megan Sumeracki, and Oliver Caviglioli

- *How Teaching Happens/How Learning Happens* by Paul Kirschner, Carl Hendrick, and Jim Heal

Thinking about the science of learning, who influences you?

Whew . . . this is tough . . . I know I'm going to leave some people out.

Pooja **Agarwal**, Patrice **Bain**, **Drs. Bjork**, Oliver **Caviglioli**, Carl **Hendrick**, Paul **Kirschner**, Henry **Roediger** III, Tom **Sherrington**, **The Learning Scientists**, Dylan **Wiliam**, Dan **Willingham**, and so many more. . .

Patrice's note: I first met Blake, online, *years* ago. *Powerful Teaching* had not yet been written, in fact, it was still simply an idea. I had been following Blake's wise blog, @ effortfuleduktr, and wrote to him asking a question. It was the first time I had ever attempted to contact one of my edu-heroes. He responded! I felt on top of the world. In 2018, we were the only K–12 teachers in the United States invited to work with cognitive scientists in Washington, D.C. with the IES (Institute of Education Sciences) and the NCER (National Center for Education Research). The mission of this working task group was to identify Neuromyths vs. Neurotruths. There have definitely been advancements in the science of learning neurotruths, which are based in research. It has certainly remained difficult to debunk some of the neuromyths. Here is Blake's blog, filled with rich ideas, items to ponder, and research: https:// theeffortfuleducator.com/. I also recommend his "Ask a Researcher" series: https://theeffortfuleducator.com/ ?s=ask+a+researcher.

DR. NINA HOOD

Location: Auckland, New Zealand

X (formerly Twitter)/LinkedIn: @hood_nina, www.linkedin .com/in/dr-nina-hood-20967058

Of your own books, articles, blogs, and/or podcasts, which is your favorite and why?

This pair of blogs – (https://theeducationhub.org.nz/living-the-science-of-learning-research/) and (https://theeducationhub.org.nz/some-considerations-around-the-science-of-learning/) – are one of my favourites. As always, my blogs are written primarily for a teacher audience and try to demonstrate what research "looks like" when applied in practice. A friend of mine wrote to me after they were published to say that publishing those two pieces simultaneously is a real commitment to nuance. To me, this captures my mission to show the value that research can offer teachers but also to encourage teachers to always question the limits of the research and what else might be needed to support their practice and the learning of their students.

The first demonstrates my own exploration of the science of learning literature in relation to my son. My son is neurodivergent, and as a result I do daily therapy/learning sessions with him. It's a fascinating exercise in seeing how the research can play out in practice, and to draw connections between what we know about how we learn and what this can look like in practice. It's also an important reminder of what Daniel Willingham says about how our brains are more similar than they are different. While there are some ways that my son's brain works that are "different," so much of the research from the science of learning applies to him.

The second blog explores some of the potential limitations of the science of learning research and in particular limitations in how it is being applied. It stems from my concern about the absolute stance that I see some in the science of learning world taking about particular approaches in education. In particular, I hope that it raises questions about other ideas and areas of research and practice that need to be considered together with the science of learning research.

Thinking of others' books, articles, blogs, and/or podcasts, what are your top three to recommend to others?

- Ollie Lovell's Education Research Reading Room podcast (https://www.ollielovell.com/podcast/) is a great podcast for teachers who are looking to hear from a wide range of education researchers and experts. In each podcast Ollie, himself a practicing teacher, interviews a different guest. There's a strong focus on the science of learning throughout the podcast episodes, but the guest speakers also come to discuss a range of areas of education and come from different philosophical perspectives. The podcast covers a wide range of topics relevant to teachers, so there's something that everyone will find interesting.

- Daniel Willingham's *Why Don't Students Like School? A Cognitive Scientist Answers Questions About How the Mind Works and What It Means for the Classroom* continues to be a book that I recommend to teachers (or gift to them), particularly if they are just starting out on their journey engaging with the science of learning research. It's such an accessible way into the cognitive science research on learning, education, and schools.

- Jared Cooney Horvath's webinar in the learning trajectory. Jared has an amazing ability to clearly and succinctly explain not only the learning process but also what this means for teachers, and why so often we seem to be talking past each other in education. In particular, Jared's discussion of why a singular focus on one part of the learning trajectory is problematic is hugely valuable for teachers to think about when planning a unit of work.

Thinking about the science of learning, who influences you?

So many people, at different times. **Daniel Willingham**, and the clear way that he communicates research has been a huge influence. **Greg Ashman** for connecting research to practice. **Tracey Tokuhama-Espinosa** for connecting me early on in my encounters with the science of learning and for connecting me with the research on the role of emotions in learning. **Ben Riley** for writing so intelligibly about New Zealand education and for bringing the science of learning to teacher education. And **Tom Sherrington** for connecting the science of learning to all aspects of teaching practice, including the curriculum.

> **Patrice's note:** I first met Nina, virtually, in 2021 and I have enjoyed our communications ever since. I have always felt warmly welcomed with her greeting: Kia ora. In 2021, I was a guest on her Education Hub webinar. Here is a video I created for Education Hub: (https://www.loom.com/share/111578790de0436a910c0c261a96ee53).

HAILI HUGHES

Location: Manchester, UK

X (formerly Twitter): @hughesHaili

Of your own books, articles, blogs, and/or podcasts, which is your favorite and why?

My book, *Mentoring in Schools*, is what has opened so many doors for me and enabled me to do wonderful things and meet incredible people. I am proud of it because it takes a fairly abstract concept and links it to cognitive science, merging both support and professional learning. It also champions experienced teachers, which of course, is so needed. In England (like in many countries) we are in the midst of a recruitment and retention crisis and research tells us that mentors are one of the most powerful tools we have in helping keep teachers in the classroom. I hope the book has helped to raise the status of mentors and support their vital work.

Thinking of others' books, articles, blogs, and/or podcasts, what are your top three to recommend to others?

- *Equity in Education* by Lee Elliot Major and Emily Briant
- *The Power of Teams* by Sam Crome
- *They Don't Behave for Me* by Sam Strickland

Thinking about the science of learning, who influences you?

Sarah Cottingham and **Efrat Furst**. I also love **Kirschner, Hendrick** and **Heal**'s book *How Teaching Happens*. It blends complex academic cognitive science theory with practical applications in the classroom. In fact, all the work Jim Heal does at Deans for Impact is brilliant. Also, **Brad Busch** and **Edward Watson**'s work at InnerDrive is amazing.

> **Patrice's note:** I had followed Haili for years on social media and had the opportunity to meet her at the Festival of Education in Maryland in 2023. Unfortunately, our presentations were at the same time so I was unable to attend her session on mentoring and coaching. Between car trips and lunches and dinners with Meg Lee, Uber rides, and the conviviality of pre- and post-conference events, it is a joy to call her my friend.

KATE JONES

Location: Birmingham, UK

X (formerly Twitter): @KateJones_Teach

Of your own books, articles, blogs, and/or podcasts, which is your favorite and why?

My favourite book is *Retrieval Practice: Primary*. This book has a specific focus on primary/elementary age learners and how teachers can introduce retrieval practice to students at a young age. I believe it is vital young children understand the importance of memory, how we learn, and why the teachers teach the

way they do – to support their learning. The sooner this understanding is grasped the better, and my book encourages primary/
elementary teachers to use effective evidence-informed strategies but also to talk to students about memory.

Thinking of others' books, articles, blogs, and/or podcasts, what are your top three to recommend to others?

- "The Model for Great Teaching." This is an evidence review published by Evidence Based Education and authored by Professor Rob Coe, Stuart Kime, C. J. Rauch, and Dan Singleton. It is a summary of research litera-ture focusing on teaching and learning, divided into four dimensions and different elements. This paper is acces-sible to all freely here: https://evidencebased.education/a-model-for-great-teaching/.

- *Strengthening the Student Toolbox: Study Strategies to Boost Learning* by Professor John Dunlosky (2013). This was an excellent summary of effective study strategies illustrating that not all revision methods are equal and students should invest their time, efforts, and energy wisely based on the evidence available (https://files.eric.ed.gov/fulltext/EJ1021069.pdf).

- Retrievalpractice.org is a fantastic website I would encourage all teachers to visit and subscribe to. Profes-sor Pooja K. Agarwal regularly updates the website with blogs, resources, research, and much more. There are free guides to download, on various topics and in different languages. All of the materials are free too! It is an incred-ibly generous, informative, and interesting source of pro-fessional learning for all teachers.

Thinking about the science of learning, who influences you?

I am influenced by those in the field of academic research such as **Daniel T. Willingham, Dylan Wiliam, Robert and Elizabeth Bjork, John Dunlosky, Pooja Agarwal,** and **Paul**

A. Kirschner. Their published work has helped me to become a better and more confident teacher in the classroom. I am also influenced and inspired by classroom teachers that share their practice and advice with others. A great example of this is **Adam Boxer**. Adam is a secondary science teacher based in London, UK, and he is also the co-founder of Carousel Learning, a digital tool to promote retrieval practice inside and outside of the classroom.

> **Patrice's note:** Kate Jones has become a legend. I originally began following Kate on social media because she was a fellow teacher who shared my passion for applying cognitive science principles and strategies with her students. I began listening to her on podcasts and each one resonated with me. In 2018, I purchased her book *Love to Teach* and then was happy to add her *Retrieval Practice* series to my bookshelf. (I was honored to write a small piece in her *Retrieval Practice 2* book.) She has since published books in the *researchED* series and the *In Action* series. Her 2023 book, *Smashing Glass Ceilings*, is aptly named for she is doing exactly that.

MARGARET "MEG" LEE

Roles: Director of Organizational Development; Author, *Mindsets for Parents*

Organization: Frederick County Public Schools

Location: Maryland, USA

X (formerly Twitter)/LinkedIn: @MegVertebrae, https://www.linkedin.com/in/margaret-lee-b36064110/

Of your own books, articles, blogs, and/or podcasts, which is your favorite and why?

I think all authors probably view their books as their "babies" to some extent because there is so much effort that goes into researching, outlining, writing, revising, and preparing the manuscript to enter the world. I'm no different, although I am most proud of the way that *Mindsets for Parents* changed between its initial publication in 2016 and the second edition in 2023. When Mary Cay Ricci and I were asked to write a second edition, we leapt at the chance because we knew so much more! My work in learning science and the journey to help my school district to become evidence-informed and equity-driven really changed my knowledge about how people learn and what impacts mindsets have (and don't have). We were able to use that evidence-informed lens to frame the guidance our book provides to parents, recognizing that mindset isn't a panacea in the classroom but holds great promise as a philosophy for adults to employ in any environment where children are present.

Thinking of others' books, articles, blogs, and/or podcasts, what are your top three to recommend to others?

Those who know me will not believe I could narrow it to three!

- *How Teaching Happens: Seminal Works in Teaching and Teacher Effectiveness and What They Mean in Practice* by Paul A. Kirschner, Carl Hendrick, and Jim Heal

- *An Everyone Culture* by Robert Kegan and Lisa Lahey

- Retrievalpractice.org, and in particular, the diverse, powerful women who are highlighted as cognitive scientists and who share their incredible expertise!

Thinking about the science of learning, who influences you?

Another very tough question! 😵

- My own "home team" of **Frederick County Public Schools' educators** – I love working with them and thinking about learning, and how to improve it for every student and every adult, every day.

- My researchED family – **Tom Bennett, Hélène Galdin-O'Shea,** and educators all over the world who give so freely of their time, talent, and treasure to help teachers and leaders be more informed about research and its application in schools.

- My dear friends at the Center for Transformative Teaching and Learning, led by **Glenn Whitman** and **Dr. Ian Kelleher**. Collaboration with them has opened up a world of opportunity and learning with colleagues near and far.

- My brain brother, **Dr. Jim Heal**, who helps me to ponder the big questions about teaching and learning, and through whom I now know so many others who have had a profound impact on my thinking, namely **Dr. Carl Hendrick**, **Dr. Paul Kirschner**, **Robin Macpherson**, and **Dr. Dan Rosen**.

Patrice's note: I met Meg when she attended a presentation I gave at researchED Philadelphia in 2019. We had an instant connection as our mutual desire for evidence-informed teaching and learning took center stage. I began working with the faculty at Frederick County Public Schools (FCPS) virtually and in-person and I always felt warmly embraced. Meg led the charge for FCPS to host researchED in 2022. Dr. Pooja Agarwal and I were the keynote speakers. Meg is a great connector of people and ideas and quick to give credit to others. I am grateful to call her a dear friend.

I was honored to do a pre-publication read of her latest book, *Mindsets for Parents*, second edition. Here is the praise I wrote for this book:

> Often a simple change in what we do reaps great rewards. Lee and Ricci illustrate how a switch from "people praise" to "process praise" leads to increased motivation, acceptance of new challenges, and the realization that errors are simply roadmaps pointing to the direction of learning as the "power of yet" is embraced. As teachers and parents, isn't this the mindset we hope for our children?

MARK McDANIEL

Role: Professor of Psychological and Brain Sciences

Organization: Washington University

Location: St. Louis, Missouri, USA

Of your own books, articles, blogs, and/or podcasts, which is your favorite and why?

Make It Stick: The Science of Successful Learning (2014). It's my favorite because it accurately conveys and summarizes a wealth of evidence and themes from well-conducted scientific studies, and it presents that information in a way that is digestible and accessible to everybody. And I think that many people find the book interesting and helpful for their learning and teaching challenges.

McDaniel and Einstein (2020). "Training learning strategies to promote self-regulation and transfer: The knowledge, belief, commitment, and planning framework." *Perspectives on Psychological Science* 15, 1363–1381.

This paper reflects a primary focus of mine in the past several years. I've developed a theoretically based operational framework for how to teach effective learning strategies to students so that they sustain self-regulation of these strategies in various classes and across semesters. In various projects we now are implementing this framework to train effective learning strategies for college students and high-school students, and have plans to begin a project with 7th-grade students. The idea is to equip students with the learning skills needed to thrive at learning, and consequently to enjoy and do well in school.

Thinking of others' books, articles, blogs, and/or podcasts, what are your top three to recommend to others?

- *Learning as a Generative Activity: Eight Learning Strategies that Promote Understanding.* Fiorella, L. and Mayer, R. E. (2015). Cambridge University Press.

- *In Their Own Words: What Scholars Want You to Know About Why and How to Apply the Science of Learning in Your Academic Setting.* Overson, C. et al. (eds.) (2023). Society for the Teaching of Psychology. https://teachpsych .org/ebooks/itow (This book is a free e-book that can be downloaded from the site.)

- *Outsmart Your Brain: Why Learning Is Hard and How You Can Make It Easy.* Willingham, D. (2023).

Thinking about the science of learning, who influences you?

There is a cadre of relatively young researchers who are energetically advancing the science of learning with well-conducted experimental studies and studies conducted in authentic educational contexts. Their work is informative and innovative. Some of these include (but not a complete list): **Andrew Butler, Shana Carpenter, Paulo Carvalho, Steven Pan, Veronica Yan,** and more.

> **Patrice's note:** The research would not have occurred in my classroom and *Powerful Teaching* would never have been written if it hadn't been for Mark McDaniel.
>
> I have frequently stated that it was at a serendipitous meeting when I had the good fortune to meet Dr. McDaniel. But there is so much more to the story (and a good one, at that!); the time is right to tell the story . . .
>
> The story begins over 50 years ago. Two young men, Mark McDaniel and Steven Bain, were attending Oberlin College in Oberlin, Ohio. During winter term, they decided to learn how to scuba dive in Jamaica. While there, they both purchased hand-carved wooden, life-sized Rastafarian heads. Fast forward to the year 2005. Steven and Mark had lost touch; Steven had married Patrice Murphy (me!) and we lived outside St. Louis, Missouri. In the *Oberlin Alumni* magazine, Steven saw that Mark was moving to St. Louis to conduct research at Washington University.

He contacted Mark and we decided to all meet at a small, quaint French restaurant for dinner. Because so much time had passed, Steven wondered if they would recognize each other. The solution? Bring the life-sized Rastafarian head! Apparently great minds think alike because at the appointed time, in walked Mark McDaniel, carrying *his* Rastafarian head! We enjoyed a wonderful French meal at a small table flanked by two masterpieces staring at us.

At dinner, Mark discussed his research on memory. I discussed teaching. And it was this serendipitous meeting, over 40 years in the making, that changed my entire teaching career.

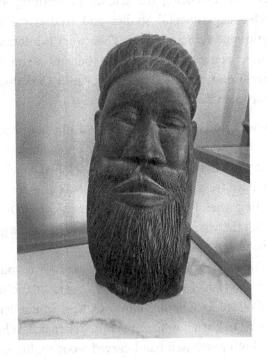

ROSS McGILL

Location: West Yorkshire, UK

X (formerly Twitter): @TeacherToolkit

Of your own books, articles, blogs, and/or podcasts, which is your favorite and why?

Guide to Memory = exploring more about how we learn. Anatomically has significantly changed how I approach teaching. It's probably the most important thing I have had to teach myself.

Thinking of others' books, articles, blogs, and/or podcasts, what are your top three to recommend to others?

- The books that have really inspired me are *Connecting the Dots* by Tricia Taylor and *Powerful Teaching* by Pooja Agarwal and Patrice Bain. I have been reading and listening to the brilliant Learning Scientists for almost a decade.

- Top recommendation is *How Learning Happens and How Teaching Happens* by Carl Hendrick and Paul Kirschner. This book is a treasure trove.

- My second top is to access Google Scholar for FREE and set up alerts on topics that you're interested in plus you can always keep up-to-date with new research.

Thinking about the science of learning, who influences you?

There are one or two people who really inspire me. First, Professor **Sarah-Jayne Blakemore**. Secondly, any neuroscientist and cognitive psychologist. I've become so deep into my own reading and thinking that I now read as many audiobooks as I can, as well as access research on a weekly basis to help generate new ideas and content for my own website.

At the heart of everything, it's when teachers suck up all the ideas and get really inspired. It reminds me of what I used to be like when I was on the front line. Many teachers feel a bit lonely, or a bit of a geek, for wanting to read up on teaching and learning on top of their day job. There are an enormous number of people in the profession who are desperate to keep learning. It is these people who are supporting many others in the profession.

Patrice's note: Ross Morrison McGill is another person I began following on social media years ago. He founded @TeacherToolkit back in 2010 and his site, https://www.teachertoolkit.co.uk/, is filled with valuable resources. Because of his vast teaching experience, he understands how busy teachers are and his site has powerful information in bite-sized chunks; often reading time can be done within two minutes. His website received the Best Education Blog at the Vuelio Blog Awards 2015, and is now reaching over 19 million readers.

Ross has written several books and among my favorites is *The Teacher Toolkit Guide to Memory* (2022). I was honored to be asked to write the Foreword and to play a role in Ross's book launch. Here is an excerpt I wrote in the Foreword:

> I agree with Ross McGill when he advocates, "All teachers must be research-informed."

The future of our profession lies in methods proven – by science – to achieve the results we want for our students. *The Teacher Toolkit Guide to Memory* boosts us into that future by sharing the *how* and *why* of learning and memory. We are better teachers when we understand concepts and questions such as the difference between our students' working and long-term memory. What do neurons and synapses have to do with their learning? How does retrieval, and spaced retrieval, strengthen knowledge retention? Dual coding, chunking, the forgetting curve, cognitive load theory . . . it's all here in this book, ready to help us boost learning in our classrooms. Understanding the science of learning makes us better teachers. As Daniel Willingham states in his book, *Why Don't Students Like School?*, "Education makes better minds, and knowledge of the mind can make better education."

I also was a guest on his podcast, Teacher Toolkit: Research Informed Retrieval Practice with Patrice Bain, and here is the link: https://www.teachertoolkit.co.uk/2019/11/17/podcast-62/?

fbclid=IwAR3ks0KsllZiH2W65FBMsGe6EY58tLjBXe8167W5Q
9AAKPTFY6vF1fVVUyY.

KAREN McINTUSH

Roles: Postdoctoral Research Fellow and Faculty Advisor

Organization: University of Houston

Location: Houston, Texas, USA

X (formerly Twitter)/LinkedIn: @kmcintush, www.linkedin
.com/in/karen-mcinstush/

**Of your own books, articles, blogs, and/or podcasts, which is
your favorite and why?**

Much of my research has focused around pre-service and novice teacher development. A recent book chapter, "Leaving so
soon? Reality shock among novice teachers" (2024) was a qualitative case study of three teachers from varied life and teaching
experiences. The findings shared resonate not only with novice
teachers, but also experienced ones due to the increased bur-
dens on teachers and rapid exit from the profession.

My recent research on classroom management is where my
passion lies. We teach a course that is community-based and
culturally responsive to secondary teacher candidates seeking secondary teacher certification. The preparation from
this course has improved their overall teacher presence and
confidence as they enter the Title I schools in the greater
Houston (Texas) area and beyond. That being said, my initial article on classroom management and diversity was published in *Learning Environments Research*, titled: "Equitable or
equal classroom management? Teacher candidates' contrasting beliefs about the impact of student demographics" (2020).
https://www.researchgate.net/publication/343899034_
Equitable_or_equal_classroom_management_Teacher_
candidates'_contrasting_beliefs_about_the_impact_of_student_
demographics

I have other publications in progress on the work with the classroom management course, but they have not yet been published.

Other favorites include three articles (one in review) that examined teachers' experiences across the state of Texas during and post-COVID-19:

- "Teaching through crisis: The remote education experiences during COVID-19 campus closures." *Technology, Pedagogy and Education* (Keese, McIntush, and Waxman, 2022) 31, 313–329.

- "From the frying pan to the fire: A qualitative analysis of teacher experiences as schools emerge from COVID-19 closures." *Social Sciences and Humanities Open* (Keese, McIntush, and Waxman, 2024) 9, 100787.

- "The road back to normal? A longitudinal qualitative investigation of teacher experiences" (Keese and McIntush, 2023).

Thinking of others' books, articles, blogs, and/or podcasts, what are your top three to recommend to others?

I enjoy and relate to posts from Tom Bennett, Tom Sherrington, and Doug Lemov. I recommend *Teach Like a Champion* (Lemov), *Conscious Discipline* (Bailey), and *Why Don't Students Like School?* (Willingham).

Thinking about the science of learning, who influences you?

The Learning Scientists, Carl Hendrick, and the many who are involved with **ResearchED.**

> **Patrice's note:** I first met Karen in 2022 when she was a Research Specialist at Texas A&M. She kindly reached out to have me work with students at the University.

MATT MILLER

Roles: Educator, Speaker, Author, Creator of *Ditch That Textbook*

Location: Tangier, Indiana, USA

X (formerly Twitter): @jmattmiller

Of your own books, articles, blogs, and/or podcasts, which is your favorite and why?

I'm really proud of my book *Tech Like a Pirate*. It's all about student engagement with technology. We published it during the pandemic – at a time when teachers were struggling with technology and trying to find a way for students to enjoy learning again. The concepts and ideas in the book have helped teachers and students to enjoy learning, and that's very rewarding to me.

Thinking of others' books, articles, blogs, and/or podcasts, what are your top three to recommend to others?

- Of course, I'm a huge fan of *Powerful Teaching*! It's such a practical guide that helps educators understand the science of learning and apply it in ways that support students.

- I've been influenced a LOT by *Teach Like a Pirate* by Dave Burgess (so much so that I wrote *Tech Like a Pirate*, the techy follow-up to his book!). I'm a huge proponent of engaging students and meeting them where they are in learning, and this book has helped me.

- I'm always learning something from Edutopia. Their articles are written by such a diverse set of educators and are always backed by research and best practice (https://www.edutopia.org/).

Thinking about the science of learning, who influences you?

Definitely **Patrice Bain** and **Pooja Agarwal**! It feels like everything I've learned about the science of learning has come from them – and from the RetrievalPractice.org website. I'm also a big fan of **The Learning Scientists**. They share such practical and understandable content.

Patrice's note: If you, like me, struggle to keep up with the latest technology, allow Matt Miller into your inbox. His site, https://ditchthattextbook.com/, is one on which I rely. Being a fellow educator, Matt understands the time limitations that face us. His emails are quick, easy to understand, and focus on what will help us in our classrooms. He sifts through mountains of technology options freeing us to apply what will benefit our students and our time. Matt also hosts a "Ditch Summit" each December to early January. This gem features Matt interviewing a wide range of educators, and technology and certificates for professional development are given. From new interviews to all previous guests, all are available during the Summit. Matt and I have presented at the same conferences, had many conversations, and, yes, he really does incorporate *Powerful Teaching* in his work!

BARBARA OAKLEY

Role: Distinguished Professor of Engineering

Organization: Oakland University

Location: Rochester, Michigan, USA

LinkedIn: www.linkedin.com/in/barbaraoakley/

Of your own books, articles, blogs, and/or podcasts, which is your favorite and why?

My favorite of all creations I've been involved in is the Uncommon Sense Teaching specialization on Coursera (https://www

.coursera.org/specializations/uncommon-sense-teaching-certificate), all about how to teach well. It grows from an understanding of how the brain works, as do most of my books and online courses.

Thinking of others' books, articles, blogs, and/or podcasts, what are your top three to recommend to others?

- *Powerful Teaching: Unleash the Science of Learning* by Pooja K. Agarwal and Patrice M. Bain

- *Make It Stick* by Peter Brown, Henry Roediger III, and Mark A. McDaniel

- *Ultralearning: Master Hard Skills, Outsmart the Competition, and Accelerate Your Career* by Scott Young

Thinking about the science of learning, who influences you?

I love to listen to the podcasts of neuroscientist **Andrew Huberman**. He provides deep insights into what is happening within our brain – much of it surprisingly relevant to the science of learning.

Google Scholar is my second "go-to" for insights about learning. I set it up to send me the newest articles about concepts like "default mode network" and "working memory," or about favorite neuroscientists like **Ran R. Hassin** and **Jonathan Schooler**, and every day is a feast.

> **Patrice's note:** Barbara Oakley is one of those rare individuals who is able to take complex information and make it accessible and relatable for all. Conducting a search of her courses at Coursera.org illustrates my previous statement. Barbara is generous in giving praise. Her review of *Powerful Teaching* – "If we had to select a single book to recommend to instructors of any kind, it would be this masterpiece – the best book on teaching that we've ever read" – has been a highlight.

SARAH OBERLE

Location: Newark, Delaware, USA

X (formerly Twitter: @S_Oberle

Of your own books, articles, blogs, and/or podcasts, which is your favorite and why?

My current favorite is the interview I did with Cindy Nebel for The Learning Scientists podcast. I really like this one because I got to discuss what it's like living in the space between research and practice, and with the challenges I've experienced during my efforts to mediate the two worlds. (https://www .learningscientists.org/learning-scientists-podcast/2023/8/31 /episode-76-meeting-at-the-intersection-of-research-and-education?rq=sarah%20oberle)

Thinking of others' books, articles, blogs, and/or podcasts, what are your top three to recommend to others?

- Brain Science podcast with Dr. Ginger Campbell (I curated a list of episodes for educators, which is on her site). https://brainsciencepodcast.com/for-educators

- *The Hobbolog* by Mike Hobbiss: Mike is a former teacher and now a researcher studying attention and cognitive control. His experience in the classroom leaves him familiar with just how critical these topics are for educators. Mike makes the research accessible for practitioners, supporting their professional judgment with knowledge about how students learn.

- *How We Learn: The New Science of Education and the Brain* by Stanislas Dehaene: If you're deeply intrigued by the mechanisms of learning and eager to leverage that understanding to enhance your teaching, then this book is tailored for you!

Thinking about the science of learning, who influences you?

Peps McCrea: love his "evidence snacks" emails with quick, digestible research tidbits (https://snacks.pepsmccrea.com/).
Jared Cooney Horvath makes research accessible with translation videos.
ResearchEd!

> **Patrice's note:** Sarah and I connected over social media and had the opportunity to meet in person at researchED Maryland in 2022. We met up again at the Festival of Education in 2023. Connecting with Sarah is like finding another science of learning kindred spirit. In addition to her doctoral studies, Sarah was the event planner and coordinator for the fabulous researchED Delaware, 2024.

JADE PEARCE

Location: Staffordshire, UK

X (formerly Twitter): @PearceMrs

Of your own books, articles, blogs, and/or podcasts, which is your favorite and why?

My book, *What Every Teacher Needs to Know: How to Embed Evidence-informed Practice in Your School*, is what I am most proud of. The aim of the book was to make evidence-informed practice (EIP) accessible to all teachers and to aid the implementation of EIP in schools across the country. I would like to think that the book's three sections – part one that summarizes 20 seminal research papers, part two that summarizes the research into key evidence-based teaching strategies and explains how these loom in the classroom, and part three that discusses how school leaders can embed EIP into their schools – achieve this aim. With 200 separate references it is packed full of educational research, at least!

Thinking of others' books, articles, blogs, and/or podcasts, what are your top three to recommend to others?

- *Putting Staff First* by John Tomsett and Jonny Uttley is my favorite leadership book, giving a blueprint for ethical leadership – how we can lead effectively and get the best for our pupils whilst putting our staff first.

- *Teach Like a Champion* by Doug Lemov gives so many practical strategies for all aspects of effective teaching from behavior management, to questioning, to participation.

- *Powerful Teaching* by Pooja Agarwal and Patrice Bain gives a brilliant explanation of the main strategies from cognitive science, including how they can be implemented in the classroom (and I promise I am not recommending this because of you, Patrice – it really is one of my favorites!).

Thinking about the science of learning, who influences you?

Brad Busch/InnerDrive – amazing blogs on all things Cog Sci! **Tom Sherrington/*WalkThrus*** – super-clear on how to implement the principles of cognitive science in the classroom.

All of the amazing teachers that I see working to implement the findings from the science of learning in their classrooms every day.

Patrice's note: After following Jade on social media, it was my absolute pleasure to meet her in person in 2021. We were both presenting at researchED Surrey in Farnham, UK. To my delight (and she did not know that I would be attending her session) *Powerful Teaching* was frequently mentioned. She has generously recommended my book over the years. Her generosity does not end there; she frequently shares strategies and insights to all. I took a look at my bookmarks on X (formerly Twitter) and the majority of items I have saved were brilliant posts from Jade! Jade has been featured in Inner

Drive's webinars and podcasts. Here is a link to Teaching and Learning Spotlight with Jade Pearce (https://www.youtube .com/watch?v=UA12ATrPNK4). Check out her writing and webinars and follow her as she graciously shares many resources.

BRUCE ROBERTSON

Location: Scotland, UK

X (formerly Twitter): @Bruce_NextLevel

Of your own books, articles, blogs, and/or podcasts, which is your favorite and why?

The Teaching Delusion 2: Teaching Strikes Back, because I think it pulls together a lot of complex ideas relating to knowledge/ skills, curriculum, pedagogy (including assessment), independent learning, and school leadership. That said, I think the most practical and useful book for teachers is *Power Up Your Pedagogy: The Illustrated Handbook of Teaching*. So, perhaps on reflection, my favorite is a tie.

Thinking of others' books, articles, blogs, and/or podcasts, what are your top three to recommend to others?

- *Teach Like A Champion 3.0* by Doug Lemov
- *Rosenshine's Principles in Action* by Tom Sherrington
- *Cognitive Load Theory in Action* by Oliver Lovell
- (But a shout-out to *Powerful Teaching*, which is also great!)

Thinking about the science of learning, who influences you?

- **Daniel T. Willingham**
- **Paul Kirschner**
- **Carl Hendrick**

Patrice's note: For years, the term "power up" was a phrase I often used whether it was in my classroom, my book *Powerful Teaching*, or my presentations. Imagine my surprise when

I heard there was a book being written called *Power Up Your Pedagogy* (2023). To my delight, I was asked to do a prepublication read. Bruce's book felt familiar; his ideas and mine complemented each other.

Here are my thoughts found in the "Praise for *Power Up Your Pedagogy*" in Bruce's book:

> Thanks to robust research, we know the importance of incorporating retrieval, spaced practice, interleaving, and feedback into our pedagogy. Robertson takes us beyond the research and shows us how to implement these principles in our classrooms. Each chapter includes Summary Charts which offer guidance, Reflective Tasks which encourage retrieval, and Finola Wilson's sketchnotes which give us screenshot captures of the material for our memory. As stated in the book, "*You* are the teacher. *You* are responsible for the conditions, the ethos, and the quality of teaching." With *Power Up Your Pedagogy*, you will have the tools to meet and exceed these responsibilities *and* have a classroom filled with successful learning. Power Up!

HENRY L. "RODDY" ROEDIGER

Role: James S. McDonnell Distinguished University Professor

Organization: Washington University

Location: St. Louis, Missouri, USA

Of your own books, articles, blogs, and/or podcasts, which is your favorite and why?

- Brown, P.C., Roediger, H.L., and McDaniel, M.A. (2014). *Make It Stick: The Science of Successful Learning*. Cambridge, MA: Harvard University Press. Translated into Arabic, Chinese (both complex and simple character translations), Czech, French, French for Africa and Haiti, German, Japanese, Korean, Polish, Portuguese, Romanian, Russian, Spanish, Turkish, Ukrainian, and Vietnamese.

- Roediger, H.L., Putnam, A.L., and Smith, M.A. (2011). Ten benefits of testing and their applications to educational practice. In *The Psychology of Learning and Motivation: Advances in Research and Theory* (eds J.P. Mestre and B.H. Ross) 1–36. Oxford: Elsevier.

- Roediger, H.L. and Butler, A.C. (2011). The critical role of retrieval practice in long-term retention. *Trends in Cognitive Sciences* 15: 20–27.

- Roediger, H.L. and Karpicke, J.D. (2006). Test-enhanced learning: Taking memory tests improves long-term retention. *Psychological Science* 17: 249–255.

- Roediger, H.L. and Karpicke, J.D. (2006). The power of testing memory: Basic research and implications for educational practice. *Perspectives on Psychological Science* 1: 181–210.

Thinking of others' books, articles, blogs, and/or podcasts, what are your top three to recommend to others?

There are too many to list here, but especially papers and chapters by the people listed below. I don't often listen to podcasts or read blogs, unless someone recommends something in particular to me.

Thinking about the science of learning, who influences you?

Mark McDaniel, Kathleen McDermott, Robert and Elizabeth Bjork, John Dunlosky, Katherine Rawson, Janet Metcalfe, Elizabeth Marsh, Hal Pashler, Richard Mayer, Shana Carpenter, Jeff Karpicke, Andrew Butler, Pooja Agarwal, Jason Chan, Karl Szpunar, Sean Kang, Veronica Yan, Nate Kornell, Magdalena Abel.

And many others that I am forgetting as I write this note.

> **Patrice's note:** Dr. Roediger is one of the kindest, most unassuming people I've ever worked with. Although he is known worldwide for his amazing research, the title he chose for me to use was "Roddy." It was a joy to join him as a guest on a St. Louis National Public Radio broadcast. We were also joined by one of my students, Zoe Hejna. Here is a recording of Dr. Henry Roediger and Patrice Bain: Are You Studying Effectively: https://www.stlpr.org/show/st-louis-on-the-air/ 2014-06-03/are-you-studying-effectively-what-wash-us-science-of-memory-tells-us-about-the-best-way-to-learn.

NIDHI SACHDEVA

Roles: Educator, Evidence-informed Learning Designer, EdTech Researcher

Organization: Ontario Institute for Studies in Education, University of Toronto, Canada

LinkedIn: https://www.linkedin.com/in/nidhi-sachdeva-toronto/

Of your own books, articles, blogs, and/or podcasts, which is your favorite and why?

That would be my doctoral dissertation titled "Designing evidence-informed microlearning for graduate level online courses." The journey I took to write that dissertation was truly a transformative experience, one that opened up the world of science of learning for me – the world in which the likes of John Sweller, Robert Bjork, Paul Kirschner, Daniel Willingham, Pooja Agarwal, Barbara Oakley, and many more amazing thinkers freely roam and share their knowledge with everyone. I initially began with the idea to explore the role of microlearning within formal higher education but during the process I realized that it's not so much whether there is a role for microlearning in academia but what we can do with it if we did it right, and by right I mean aligning the design of microlearning content with the principles from cognitive science. If I was allowed to choose more than one, I'd also say my blog titled "Science of Learning" that I co-author with Dr. Jim Hewitt. It's very dear to us and we focus on reducing the gap between educational research and practice by simplifying the messaging for practicing educators.

Thinking of others' books, articles, blogs, and/or podcasts, what are your top three to recommend to others?

- **Podcast:** "Chalk and Talk" by Anna Stokke: Stokke does a tremendous job of simplifying many concepts from the science of learning and what that means for instructional practice. There is a strong focus on math instruction but the discussions with guests on the podcast provide valuable insights to all educators. It also does something unique for educators and that is it reminds them to ask the question – what's the evidence in support of "so and so" practice? https://chalkandtalkpodcast.podbean.com/

- **Book:** *How Learning Happens* by Paul Kirschner and Carl Hendrick. I love this text because it has reignited the discussion about the greatest hits from educational research and what it means for educational practice. It addresses many themes like how novices learn and how experts learn, what's the role of prior knowledge, how dual coding theory can settle the debate that learning styles are a myth, how we could reach many more learners if we followed what Barak Rosenshine called "direct instruction/principles of instruction" and so much more. I have developed a series of videos that align with this book – "How Learning Happens – Cognitive Load and Problem Solving" (https://www.youtube.com/watch?v=aMSmHOYkGcQ).

- **Article:** "Principles of Instruction" by Barak Rosenshine. Research-based strategies that all teachers should know published in the *American Educator* in 2012. This article is a golden piece of writing. Rosenshine's principles bring many theoretical foundations from the science of learning in the form of ten principles that are beneficial for every educator to know and apply.

Thinking about the science of learning, who influences you?

The list is long but I will mention some names here (not an exhaustive list by any means):

- **Patrice Bain**
- **Barak Rosenshine**'s work
- **John Sweller**
- **Paul Kirschner**
- **Carl Hendrick**
- **Robert Bjork**
- **Daniel Willingham**
- **Henry Roediger**
- **Pooja Agarwal**
- **Barbara Oakley**
- **Keith Stanovich**
- **Greg Ashman**
- **John Mighton**
- Folks at **The Learning Scientists: Megan Sumeracki, Cynthia Nebel**
- **Amanda VanDerHeyden**

Patrice's note: Much to my delight, I received a message from Nidhi in 2023 stating she would like to connect and would

I be open to a conversation? We had much in common, a friendship developed, and more conversations continued. Nidhi and I share a common passion: Bring parents into the science of learning conversation. Nidhi chaired the fabulous international event: researchED Toronto in May 2024, which once again, brought together many of the people featured in this book.

TOM SHERRINGTON

Location: London, UK

X (formerly Twitter): @teacherhead

Of your own books, articles, blogs, and/or podcasts, which is your favorite and why?

Teaching WalkThrus US Edition, co-authored with Oliver Caviglioli, brings together the highlights of our original volumes 1–3, representing a distillation of ideas about teaching and learning that I'm very proud of. The five-step visual guide to over 100 strategies has proven to be popular with practising teachers and, ultimately, they are the people who really matter. The "why" section includes summaries of ideas from Willingham, Wiliam, Rosenshine, and more, linked to a clear learning model. It's that connection between theory and practice that I think is so important.

Thinking of others' books, articles, blogs, and/or podcasts, what are your top three to recommend to others?

In my training sessions, I normally include the following three:

- Dan Willingham's *Why Don't Students Like School?*
- Barak Rosenshine's *Principles of Instruction: Research-Based Strategies All Teachers Should Know*
- Sarah Cottingham's *Ausubel's Meaningful Learning in Action* from the *In Action* series.

Thinking about the science of learning, who influences you?

My influencers are **Dan Willingham** and **Dylan Wiliam**, who bring such depth and clarity. Willingham on the core architecture of memory and the importance of thinking; Wiliam on formative assessment and the challenges of feedback, linking the science to classroom dynamics. In the space of memory and meaning-making the work of **Megan Sumeracki**, **Efrat Furst**, and **Sarah Cottinghatt** has helped me understand the role of individual students engaging in elaborative interrogation, prediction, and mental rehearsal, linking to prior knowledge. **Fiorella and Mayer's** work on "Generative Learning" and **Rosenshine's** "Principles of Instructions" are useful counterparts, both linking theory to practice in a complementary manner. **Graham Nuthall's** *Hidden Lives of Learners* is a gem of a book that explores the realities teachers and students face in real classrooms. Finally, the key blogger–teacher who has influenced me is **David Didau**, who is brilliant at challenging misconceptions and applying ideas to English teaching and teaching in general.

> **Patrice's note:** Tom Sherrington is another one of my edu-heroes I had been following for years. I was delighted to find out that we would be presenting at the same conference, researchED Surrey (Farnham, UK) in 2021 and couldn't wait to sit in on his talk. (By the way, this conference was held at the same school where Tom's mother had worked.) I clearly remember walking down the hallway and seeing him. To my absolute surprise, he turned around and exclaimed, "Patrice Bain!" and wanted a selfie. This minute in time became known to me as a "Tom Sherrington Moment!" In my mind, I will always be the teacher from a small town in Illinois; I continue to be surprised when people know who I am. From that time on, whenever I am recognized, it becomes another "Tom Sherrington Moment!" I have been fortunate to see him at other conferences since

then and was even present at an evening event during the 2022 researchED (put together by Meg Lee and her Frederick County Public Schools team) where he and Tom Bennett made their first American s'mores!

Here is the testimonial I wrote for the US Edition for *Walk-Thru 5-Step Guides to Build Great Teaching*:

New teacher? Instructional Coach? Veteran Teacher? *WalkThru* is for ALL of us! This book practices what it preaches – breaking down learning and best practices into manageable chunks and offering dual coding to help us commit it to memory. Bravo Sherrington and Caviglioli!

Tom and Emma Turner host a wonderful podcast called Mind the Gap:
https://teacherhead.com/2022/12/24/mind-the-gap-a-lovely-year-for-our-emma-and-tom-show-thanks-for-listening/.

Here is the episode where I was the guest called Mind the Gap, Episode 14, Powerful Teaching for All with Patrice Bain:

(https://podcasts.apple.com/us/podcast/episode-14-powerful-teaching-for-all-with-patrice-bain/id151653253 7?i=1000501693481)

DR. ANNA STOKKE

Role: Professor

Location: Winnipeg, Manitoba, Canada

X (formerly Twitter): @rastokke

Of your own books, articles, blogs, and/or podcasts, which is your favorite and why?

My podcast, "Chalk and Talk." Why? I interview leading researchers and educators on evidence-based teaching methods. I believe it is most impactful because it has reached many teachers, parents, and educators who have contacted me to let me know how helpful it is.

Thinking of others' books, articles, blogs, and/or podcasts, what are your top three to recommend to others?

- Daniel Willingham: *Outsmart Your Brain*
- Barbara Oakley: *A Mind for Numbers*
- John Mighton: *The End of Ignorance*
- Podcast: "Hidden Brain"

Thinking about the science of learning, who influences you?

Greg Ashman, Tom Bennett, Zach Groshell, Carl Hendrick, Paul Kirschner, John Mighton, Barbara Oakley, Amanda VanDerHeyden

> Patrice's note: Anna's "Chalk and Talk" podcast is a great one. She interviews a variety of people and is always able to tie in a math focus. Here is the link: https://chalkandtalkpodcast. podbean.com. I had the pleasure of being one of Anna's guests and here is the link for our chat, Chalk and Talk, Episode 13 with Patrice Bain, *Powerful Teaching* with a math focus: https://chalkandtalkpodcast.podbean.com/e/ep-13-powerful-teaching-with-patrice-bain/.

MAREK TKACZYK

Location: Opole, Poland

LinkedIn: https://www.linkedin.com/in/marek-tkaczyk-408b5422/

Of your own books, articles, blogs, and/or podcasts, which is your favorite and why?

My webinar I did a few years ago for an American TESOL institute. In about 100 minutes I demonstrate, using popular coursebooks and teaching materials, how I implement Retrieval Practice and Lexical Approach in foreign language classes and show practical ways of increasing the efficiency of learning and teaching. It was during the preparation process for this webinar when I realised that almost all the effective teaching tools and techniques I'd been using for ages had one common factor: They were all based on Retrieval Practice and/or Metacognition and hence their powerful teaching. Link: https://youtu.be/11Zc4gOFaYA?feature=shared

Thinking of others' books, articles, blogs, and/or podcasts, what are your top three to recommend to others?

- *Learning Teaching* by Jim Scrivener – an absolute must-read book for all language teachers.

- "A conversation about language acquisition" – a webinar in which a hyperpolyglot Steven Kaufmann talks with Dr. Stephen Krashen about the most effective tools and techniques that speed up foreign language acquisition (https://www.youtube.com/watch?v=p7WUxvpPIKQ).

- "How to learn a new language with stories" – Olly Richards explains how to acquire a new language mostly by reading stories (https://www.youtube.com/watch?v=dPqWN2dlsBg).

Thinking about the science of learning, who influences you?

As my field of expertise is foreign languages, my main influences come from top linguists and hyperpolyglots. My gurus in this field are **Stephen Krashen, Olly Richards, Scott Thornbury, Jeremy Harmer,** and **Steven Kaufmann**.

> **Patrice's note:** Marek contacted me and asked if I would be on his webinar and it turned into quite a unique opportunity. Prior to the podcast, Marek asked me to write a letter to my favorite teacher and we would discuss it during our conversation. To write the letter, I went back in time to my high school in Sioux Falls, South Dakota, and thought about what a remarkable teacher Mrs. Hart was and how her teaching influenced me. I appreciated Marek's approach and embraced the experience to wander down memory lane. You can watch the podcast, "Powerful Language Teaching" at https://www.youtube.com/watch?v=7Q-9QHC8i3Y.

EMMA TURNER (FCCT)

Roles: Primary Education Consultant, Author, School Improvement Advisor

Location: England, UK

X (formerly Twitter)/LinkedIn: @Emma_turner75, linkedin .com/in/emma-l-turner

Of your own books, articles, blogs, and/or podcasts, which is your favorite and why?

Simplicitus: The Interconnected Primary Curriculum and Effective Subject Leadership is the book of which I am most proud as it has helped and supported so many schools and colleagues to design their curriculum and lead their subjects through the specific primary school lens. Much of what is written about education is often from a secondary/high school angle and doesn't include reference to the unique and key developmental window that is early and mid-childhood. The primary age range of 4–11 takes children from the edge of toddlerhood to the cusp of adolescence and as such needs to balance both what we know about cognitive science and what we know about child development. *Simplicitus* aimed to capture the practical "how to" and also the "why" of what we do in primary to introduce our youngest learners in the formal education system to the joy and wonder of a playful but still challenging academic curriculum. *Simplicitus* then led to the writing of *Initium* which means "Beginning." This book took principles and findings from cognitive science and again passed them through the lens of the primary school day. I am immensely proud of *Initium* for sparking discussion and reflection about what works, but also what is right for younger learners.

Drawing on my 26 years in primary, 20 of those in the classroom, *Initium* talks through how to translate cognitive science findings into provision for primary age children, allying these findings with research from child development and effective primary pedagogy. I can also be heard flying the flag for early years and primary on the "Mind the Gap" podcast which I co-host with Tom Sherrington (https://www.youtube.com/@ MindtheGapwithTomEmma). I have been so lucky to work with Tom and to listen to the warmth, wit, and wisdom of dozens of educators from across the globe. The episode with Sarah Cottingham discussing Ausubel's research into meaningful learning is a personal favourite of mine as Sarah has a gift for taking complex research and making it both accessible and fascinating (https://www.youtube.com/watch?v=ghxgRqOyin4). In all of my work I hope you can hear my immense joy and love for the primary phase jumping from every page or sentence. Working with our youngest learners is a privilege and a joy like no other and I hope that my work supports all those who choose to be educators in the receiving line stage of education as we welcome children into their academic adventures.

Thinking of others' books, articles, blogs, and/or podcasts, what are your top three to recommend to others?

Without classrooms that are calm, purposeful, and supportive, learning cannot happen effectively. With this in mind, the work of Sam Strickland will always be top of my list of initial reads. His books, *The Behaviour Manual* and *They Don't Behave for Me* are not only accessible and beautifully written but are informed by his work as an exceptional principal of a 4–18 school of 2,000 pupils. The suggestions in his book are lived out in his day-to-day work and he is a unique voice in the behaviour space not only for his precise and practical writing style but as a serving and experienced principal.

The greatest education book I have ever read and the one that will always have a special place in my heart is *The Magic-Weaving Business* by Sir John Jones. Not only is it hugely practical in helping to articulate why and how we do what we do as teachers but it focuses with precision and warmth on the "why." For anyone who is thinking of becoming a teacher, or for anyone who wants to reconnect with why they do what they do, this is essential reading. I challenge anyone to read this book and it not automatically be in their own top three of greatest-ever educational reads.

Primary education needs to ensure that every child leaves as a reader. The work of Christopher Such in his book *The Art and Science of Teaching Primary Reading* is, to my mind, the seminal work on this topic. It is invaluable reading for any teacher of young children and explains what can be a daunting landscape of research with precision and clarity. This is the book I am never more than a few feet from and I am already on my second copy!

Thinking about the science of learning, who influences you?

The work of **Efrat Furst** and **Sarah Cottingham** and their focus on the importance of connection will always be an area of fascination for me. A scientist by training, I am in thrall to their deep understanding of neuroscience, twinned with their experience as educators. They manage to bridge the gap between science and education with extraordinary dexterity and care – making even the hugely abstract and technical accessible for all.

Carl Hendrick's work on how teaching happens and how learning happens is a constant reference point for me when writing training and supporting colleagues.

Finally, I cannot fail to mention my colleague and co-host **Tom Sherrington** and his partnership with **Oliver Caviglioli** in developing the *WalkThrus* series. Their 5-step approach has meant that thousands of colleagues across the globe now have well-informed and accessible guides which help translate research into actionable approaches.

Patrice's note: It was a joy to be on the "Mind the Gap" podcast with Emma and Tom Sherrington. The link to Mind the Gap, Episode 14, Powerful Teaching for All with Patrice Bain is here: https://podcasts.apple.com/us/podcast/episode-14-powerful-teaching-for-all-with-patrice-bain/id1516532537?i=1000501693481.

Emma's personality is joyful and I can't help but smile when I see her name or when we are in communication. The first book of Emma's I read was *Be More Toddler: A Leadership Education from Our Little Learners*. I thought the book was a brilliant guide for administrators and teacher leaders.

I was delighted to be asked to do a prepublication read for her book *Initium*. Here is the praise I wrote for this outstanding book:

> Turner reminds us how easy it is, as expert learners, to fall into the "curse of knowledge," forgetting what it is like to see ourselves as primary learners and provides us a roadmap of the necessary guidance, scaffolding, and connection-making to ensure successful learning. Her writing takes us on a delightful journey illustrating how researched principles – vital to learning – can and should be used playfully, joyfully, and appropriate to the ages and stages of primary children. *Verba volant, scripta manent*: Words fly away, writings remain. Fortunately for all of us, including our youngest learners, *Initium* is here to stay. Thank you, Emma Turner, for this gift!

ANDREW WATSON

Roles: President, Translate the Brain; Blogger, Social Media Director, and Coordinator of onsite PD for Learning and the Brain

Location: Boston, Massachusetts, USA

X (formerly Twitter): AndrewWatsonTTB

Of your own books, articles, blogs, and/or podcasts, which is your favorite and why?

The Goldilocks Map – I hope – helps teachers make sense of "brain-based" teaching advice. We hear so often that "research says you should change your teaching!" But it's very difficult to know whether or not that claim has real research behind it. *TGM* offers specific strategies to answer that question – and I don't think many other books take this approach.

Thinking of others' books, articles, blogs, and/or podcasts, what are your top three to recommend to others?

- researchED conferences: the best way to get well-curated guidance from researchers who take classroom work seriously, and teachers who take research seriously.

- Dan Willingham's *Why Don't Students Like School?* I'm sure EVERYONE includes this book in their list. I'm echoing that recommendation because – honestly – most of the core guidance I offer teachers is ultimately based on his ideas, and his framing of them.

- *WalkThrus* (Sherrington and Caviglioli) includes SO MANY research-based strategies and insights, it's a handy reference for dozens (hundreds) of essential concepts.

Thinking about the science of learning, who influences you?

Christian Bokhove, Adam Boxer, Sarah Cottingham, Efrat Furst, Zac Groshell, Stuart Kime, Meg Lee, Peps Mccrea, Cindy Nebel, Sarah Oberle, Kristin Simmers, Anna Stokke.

Patrice's note: I first met Andrew Watson at researchED Philadelphia in 2019. It was my first researchED, my book had recently been published, and I knew no one. Much to my delight and relief, Andrew introduced himself and a conversation ensued. Andrew is very accomplished and knowledgeable; his wit, wisdom, and charisma are always a welcome treat . . . whether it be reading his blog, seeing him at a conference, or communicating through social media and emails. I was fortunate to be asked to do a prepublication read of his book: *The Goldilocks Map*. The charm and wit with which the book is written is a breath of fresh air not often found in educational books – *especially* ones that pertain to research. It is rare that I don't discuss this book in my presentations.

Here is the review I wrote for *The Goldilocks Map*:

It is vital for educators to ask: On what evidence is this based? Yet, do we know the validity of the answer or how to evaluate the research? How will I know if the studies being referenced apply to my students? Watson takes us on an enjoyable journey tackling the ideas we wish we had been taught in our teacher education programs. Does the research apply? Is it a waste of time? Is it worth pursuing? Watson takes us, step by step, on the path that boosts learning for our students and leads us to become better informed educators. *The Goldilocks Map* is not a fairytale; it provides teachers and administrators needed direction.

MITCH WEATHERS

Role: Founder and CEO

Organization: Organized Binder, Inc.

X (formerly Twitter): https://www.twitter.com/organizedbinder

LinkedIn: www.linkedin.com/in/mitchweathers/

Facebook: https://www.facebook.com/organizedbinder/

Instagram: https://www.instagram.com/organizedbinder/

Of your own books, articles, blogs, and/or podcasts, which is your favorite and why?

What I have discussed and published over the years has always had a bias toward action. Action in an effort to answer one question, "What has the greatest impact on student success?" I am not convinced that executive functioning skills are found at the core of the answer to this question.

From the moment I started teaching, I became obsessed with translating the research and publications I was reading on the science of learning into effective, yet practical and realistic strategies that I could implement in my classroom. But as I dove into the research, I continually asked myself, "Although this is fascinating, and I know it can help my students succeed, what does it actually *look* like in the modern classroom?"

My favorite publication to date is my first, and only, book, *Executive Functions for Every Classroom: Creating Safe and Predictable Learning Environments*. I am most proud of this work because it accomplished exactly what I set out to do all those years ago when I entered the classroom. It translates the emerging science of learning, focusing on the development of executive functioning skills to lay the foundation for success, into practical and actionable strategies teachers can realistically implement in their classroom.

I am also proud of the timing of this book. In the wake of the [COVID-19] pandemic, there has never been a more critical time to bring structure and coherence to the school experience in a way that increases student agency, particularly those students furthest from opportunity. All students benefit from participating in a predictable daily learning routine that gives them practice with the executive functioning skills that lay the foundation for learning and success.

Thinking of others' books, articles, blogs, and/or podcasts, what are your top three to recommend to others?

- *Powerful Teaching* by Agarwal and Bain
- *How Learning Happens* by Kirschner and Hendrick
- *Pedagogy of the Oppressed* by Freire

As a teacher and practitioner, I have always been interested in the science of learning. The propensity in our industry seems to be toward content standards, the "what" we teach. I understand that what we teach is important, but unless we consider how students learn, it doesn't really matter what we teach them.

I first discovered Paulo Freire's work while exploring critical theory and equity. However, he was also the first to spark my interest in the science of learning. With this one sentence, from *Pedagogy of the Oppressed*, it became undeniably clear to me that what we teach is secondary to the learning process: "Liberating education consists in acts of cognition, not transferrals of information."

Yet, I have always been empathetic toward the classroom teacher because transferring information is what we are hired to do. But if we do not simultaneously address how students learn while we focus on what we teach, our students will experience less success. This is the very reason that *Powerful Teaching* spoke to me! For any teacher interested in the science of learning who also has a conviction to make education more equitable, fair, inclusive, and empowering, *Pedagogy of the Oppressed* is a must read.

Thinking about the science of learning, who influences you?

Pooja Agarwal, Patrice Bain, Henry L. Roediger, Mark McDaniel, Peter C. Brown, Carl Hendrick, Paul A. Kirschner, to name a few.

Patrice's note: Mitch reached out to me several years ago through a mutual friend. He sent me one of his Organized Binders and it made so much sense to me. Clearly, this would help my students who often ran into class as the bell rang with papers swirling around them as if a midwestern tornado had just hit. The communication this system held was a gift for teachers, parents, and students. Fast forward to 2023. Mitch was writing his book: *Executive Functions for Every Classroom* and not only asked me if I would do a pre-read, but also if I would consider writing the Foreword! I was honored. For his book launch, Mitch held a "Thriving Educator's Summit" where once again I was honored to keynote. He chose people from a wide range of educational fields and I found myself eagerly listening to each person's expertise (https://organizedbinder.com/tes24/).

GLENN WHITMAN

Role: Dreyfuss Family Director, The Center for Transformative Teaching and Learning (CTTL)

Organization: St. Andrew's Episcopal School

Location: Potomac, Maryland, USA

X (formerly Twitter)/LinkedIn: @gwhitmancttl, https://www.linkedin.com/in/gwhitman/

Of your own books, articles, blogs, and/or podcasts, which is your favorite and why?

Without a doubt, co-authoring *Neuroteach: Brain Science and the Future of Education*, written while a classroom teacher, is my favorite because kindergarten through college teachers and school leaders find utility in its "next-day" applicable research, principles, and strategies. I have enjoyed each conversation I have while recording The CTTL's "Think Differently and Deeply" podcast with teachers, students, and school leaders (https://www.thecttl.org/podcasts/). It has also been great to see how The CTTL's Science of Teaching and School Leadership Academy (https://www.thecttl.org/) has grown to include public and private schools and district satellite sites in the United States and Mexico and that we are now in our fifth volume of our school's international publication, *Think Differently and Deeply* (https://www.thecttl.org/think-differently-deeply/), which provides a model for translating promising research and strategies into practice and has been shared with over 30,000 educators around the world.

Thinking of others' books, articles, blogs, and/or podcasts, what are your top three to recommend to others?

- The "Great Teaching Toolkit" from Evidence Based Education.
- I find Deans for Impact's *Research to Practice* publications very accessible for the everyday teacher.
- The Learning and the Brain Conferences, researchED, and Festival of Education are all "bucket list" worthy professional learning and growth experiences.
- Anything written by Mary Helen Immordino Yang or Dan Willingham.

Thinking about the science of learning, who influences you?

I draw inspiration and influence from educators and researchers who embrace the potential and advancements in the science of teaching and learning while maintaining a critical eye toward the expanding body of research and resources within the field. I am grateful for the invaluable guidance and mentorship from individuals like **Mariale Hardiman**, who served as my initial point of contact in MBE research and strategies, as well as **David Daniel, Efrat Furst, Mark McDaniel, Beth Morling, Dan Willingham, Denise Pope, Dylan Wiliam, Mary Helen Immordino Yang, Pedro de Bruckeye,** and **Tracey Tokuhama-Espinosa.** Additionally, I am continually inspired by teacher-researchers who have either transitioned from or remain actively engaged in the classroom and working with students, including **Patrice Bain, Blake Harvard, Meg Lee, Andrew Watson, Ian Kelleher, Tia Henteleff, Lorraine Martinez Hanley,** and **Kris Simmers**. Both cohorts demonstrate a commitment to sharing their knowledge and ongoing discoveries, aimed at enhancing instructional practices, school environments, and the holistic development of students within classrooms, schools, and districts.

> **Patrice's note:** I met Glenn through my friendship with Meg Lee. The Center for Transformative Teaching and Learning (CTTL), which he co-founded, has been cited several times throughout this book. The CTTL Summer Academies are outstanding; I have had the honor of being a presenter. He has been involved with, and presented, at many of the researchED conferences I have attended and he was instrumental in planning the Inaugural Festival of Education in 2023 and will also be leading future events.

ANDREW WHITWORTH

Role: Assistant Headteacher: Quality of Education

Location: Hampshire, UK

X (formerly Twitter)/LinkedIn: @whitworthtin4

Of your own books, articles, blogs, and/or podcasts, which is your favorite and why?

One-Page education summaries: Digestible research is crucial for teachers because it bridges the gap between complex educational studies and practical classroom applications. Busy teachers, who often juggle multiple responsibilities, may find it challenging to sift through dense academic papers. Summarised research provides accessible insights and evidence-based strategies that can be quickly understood and implemented. This enhances teaching practices by integrating the latest findings and methodologies and supports informed decision-making, ultimately leading to improved student outcomes. Teachers are empowered to continually evolve their instructional methods by making research digestible, fostering a more effective and responsive learning environment.

Thinking of others' books, articles, blogs, and/or podcasts, what are your top three to recommend to others?

- *Make It Stick: The Science of Successful Learning* – by Peter C. Brown et al.
- *Powerful Teaching: Unleash the Science of Learning* – by Pooja K. Agarwal and Patrice M. Bain
- *Creating the Schools our Children Need* – Dylan Wiliam

Thinking about the science of learning, who influences you?

John Sweller, Robert Bjork, David Ausubel, Henry L. Roediger, III

> **Patrice's note:** I have yet to have the opportunity to meet Andrew Whitworth in person but I feel like I have known him for years. His One Pagers resonate with me. If you aren't aware of his work, please be sure to follow him on X (formerly Twitter). He graciously shares his work and I have frequently used his resources in my presentations. His One Pagers are a gift and are welcome additions for use in professional development and classrooms. You can access them through his X account.

DANIEL WILLINGHAM

Role: Professor

Organization: University of Virginia

Location: Charlottesville, Virginia, USA

Of your own books, articles, blogs, and/or podcasts, which is your favorite and why?

Probably my book, *Outsmart Your Brain*, because I worked very hard to offer a more comprehensive guide for student success than I thought was available. It took me a long time and I feel proud of the results.

Thinking of others' books, articles, blogs, and/or podcasts, what are your top three to recommend to others?

https://characterlab.org: an amazing array of useful resources from Angela Duckworth's lab.

Ollie Lovell is a thoughtful interviewer, and has wonderful people on his podcasts: https://www.ollielovell.com/podcast/

How Learning Happens by Paul Kirschner and Carl Hendrick offers readable summaries of seminal works in educational psychology and also explains why they are so important, and their implications for educators.

Thinking about the science of learning, who influences you?

Numbers 1–4 on a list of 10 would be my wife, **Trisha Thompson-Willingham**, a teacher and administrator for 30 years.

Among scientists, **David Yeager** is an inspiration, as I think he's pioneering new methods in intervention studies that will be the norm in the coming decades.

Stan Dehaene has made original contributions to AND been a brilliant synthesizer of multiple fields, including math, reading, and learning. I'm always interested in what he is doing.

Herb Simon died in 2001, but I continue to find new insights in his prodigious body of work.

> **Patrice's note:** *Outsmart Your Brain* is an excellent book. However, my history of learning about Willingham began with *Why Students Don't Like School?* (1st Edition!) It was the first science-of-learning book I purchased, read, and reread for it resonated with me. His words and phrases became quotes I use in all of my presentations.

I first met him in 2019 at the NWAIS (Northwest Association of Independent Schools), held in Tacoma, Washington, where I presented and he was the keynote speaker. In 2021, Willingham wrote the 2nd Edition of *Why Students Don't Like School?* and I was honored to be asked to do a prepublication read. His weaving of information from earlier chapters into current chapters, allowing for retrieval, spacing, and deep understanding, is masterful. His questions at the ends of chapters are excellent and provide tools for personal reflections and understanding for those conducting book studies. The following is the endorsement I wrote for this book:

> Education makes better minds and knowledge of the mind can make better education.
>
> *Daniel Willingham*

Willingham's 2nd Edition takes us on a deeper dive into the knowledge of the mind; it takes what we now know and presents it in a way that encourages educators to hone their craft. Not only will *education be better*, but also students will benefit with the retention of long-term learning.

DR. STEPHANIE J. YEARIAN

Role: Retired Associate Professor, Dyslexia Practitioner

Location: Waterloo, Illinois, USA

Facebook: Stephanie J. Yearian

Of your own books, articles, blogs, and/or podcasts, which is your favorite and why?

"Empowerment of Teachers and Students through Innovative Literacy Practices" UMI 3474300 Copyright 2011 by ProQuest LLC: My 265-page dissertation is my favorite writing because similar to Patrice's endeavor, I interviewed 20 educators and

specialists across the nation in the field of reading, which
included the following, among others:

- Joanne Yatvin of the National Reading Panel (NRP 1997–2000).

- Dr. Michael Hefferty, author of the program *Phonemic Awareness: The Skills That They Need to Help Them Succeed!* (2010).

- Jennifer McDonough, co-author of *A Place for Wonder: Reading and Writing Nonfiction in the Primary Grades* (2009) and *Conferring with Young Writers: What to Do When You Don't What to Do* (2016).

- Alesia Hamilton and Alferd Williams, a first-grade teacher who taught 69-year-old Alferd to read, featured in *People* magazine, on "Oprah" and "Ellen."

- Beth Holland, my dear friend from my experience on the McMillian McGraw-Hill Advisory Board in New York for the Treasures curriculum (2007).

Thinking of others' books, articles, blogs, and/or podcasts, what are your top three to recommend to others?

- *The Daily Five: Fostering Literacy Independence in the Elementary Grades* (Boushey, G. and Moser, J., 2009) and *The CAFE Book: Engaging All Students in Daily Literacy Assessment & Instruction* (Boushey, G. and Moser, J., 2009) were researched and practiced in 3 out of the 14 classrooms that I observed in my sample, with the Waterloo School District (Illinois, USA) being the fourth to pick up *Daily Five* practices after my writing, which gave evidence that the theory was effective. Jennifer McDonough had developed a similar relationship with the sisters of the *Daily Five* program, Gail Boushey and Joan Moser, as did my close association with Michael Heggerty, who spoke often to my Lindenwood University teacher candidates and shared *Phonemic Awareness* programs for their future classrooms.

- The following book is my main resource for instruction on the fourth (Latin) and fifth (Greek/French) levels of tutoring in Orton-Gillingham strategies: *Unlocking Literacy: Effective Decoding and Spelling Instruction* by Marcia K. Henry.

- I continue to highly recommend Michael Heggerty's program, which is regularly updated by the company to address educational needs: *Phonemic Awareness: The Skills That They Need to Help Them Succeed!*

Thinking about the science of learning, who influences you?

Patrice Bain has influenced me in the science of learning since my master's degree, while she presented to my Reading in the Content Area classes (Lindenwood University, Belleville, Illinois, USA) and through her presentations for the Lewis and Clark Reading Council (LCRC).

What are the 5 components of the *science of reading*? They include phonemic awareness, phonics, vocabulary, fluency, and comprehension. (*The Science of Reading reiterates the findings of the National Reading Panel.*)

Orton-Gillingham (OG), which are the strategies that I use during tutoring in reading, is an instructional approach rooted in the science of reading. It was developed in the 1930s by Dr. Samuel Orton and Anna Gillingham to help students with dyslexia and other reading difficulties.

I wish that I had been trained in OG prior to teaching reading methods classes to teacher candidates for the 10 years at Lindenwood University, and the young elementary students for the 20 years prior to the university!

Patrice's note: I first met Stephanie Yearian as her professor in the first class she took as she began undertaking her master's degree. Regardless of the ages of the students in my classes, I consistently had those memorable ones who stood out due to their investment, creativity, and deep interest in the content. Stephanie met all those criteria! Years later, after she had obtained her doctorate degree and taught at a university, Dr. Yearian asked me to give presentations to her college students, which I enjoyed doing for several years. It was during that time that we became dear friends.

One of my favorite educational experiences has been observing Dr. Yearian during her tutoring sessions with dyslexic students. With each student, I was amazed at the strategies used *and* the student's understanding of the *whys* that made the strategies work. I wish *every* student who has difficulty reading had someone like Dr. Yearian in their life!

Chapter *9*

Do-It-Yourself Retrieval Guide

This Guide is for you. You may want to complete it individually, with your team, or as a book study. Take your time to retrieve, space, interleave, check your metacognition, and ponder.

CHAPTER 1: HOW IT STARTED

1. What is your background with the science of learning?

2. How might knowing about learning change your own educational trajectory?

3. What books, podcasts, webinars, articles, etc., have helped you on your learning journey?

4. If you could plan your own learning revolution, with a seat at the table, what would it look like?

CHAPTER 2: THE RESEARCH

1. Describe the research studies in Patrice Bain's classroom.

2. Did any of the results surprise you?

3. How would you design a study on learning?

CHAPTER 3: LEARNING

1. What are the three steps of learning?

2. Why is learning considered "messy"?

3. Define the Power Tools:

Retrieval:	Spacing:
Interleaving:	Feedback-driven Metacognition:

4. Why are Desirable Difficulties desirable?

5. What are some ways you can reduce cognitive overload?

6. Why is it important to have background knowledge when learning new material?

7. Give some examples of you and/or students experiencing illusions of learning.

8. Willingham says "Memory is the residue of thought." What are your thoughts on learning?

CHAPTER 4: POWER TOOLS

1. Why might retrieval, spacing, interleaving, and feedback-driven metacognition be considered Power Tools?

2. How would you describe Power Tools to a parent, a teacher, an administrator?

3. Did completing the Think and Link help increase your knowledge retention of retrieval?

4. What is the Forgetting Curve?

5. How can you lighten the Forgetting Curve through the use of spacing?

6. Think of the classes you teach or observe: Are they geared to "one and done/teach and move on" or are retrieval and spacing incorporated?

7. How would you explain interleaving?

8. Why should students use retrieval strategies throughout a course of study?

9. Why is feedback a necessary component of metacognition?

CHAPTER 5: SCHOOLS AND CONFERENCES

1. What types of professional development are available to you?

2. How would you design professional development?

3. You are in charge of a "Dream Big Conference." Describe it.

4. When attending conferences or webinars, or listening to podcasts, what do you hope to take away?

CHAPTER 6: STRATEGIES

1. You are tasked with creating a document of Common Instructional Strategies for a school. What will you include?

2. Many strategies were offered. What are your top three for each of the Power Tools?

Retrieval:	Spacing:
Interleaving:	Metacognition:

3. Patrice listed eight criteria she used for creating strategies. What would be your criteria for developing strategies based on the Power Tools?

4. Create an infographic for Power Tools.

CHAPTER 7: TEACHERS AND LEADERS

This chapter was filled with strategies and ideas for implementing the science of learning into schools and professional development.

1. Specific strategies I would like to try:

2. Specific strategies for professional development:

3. You may already be doing some of what was highlighted in this chapter. In the chart, what are some things or strategies you would like to start, what are some you'd like to stop, and what are you already doing that you want to make sure you keep?

Start	Stop	Keep

CHAPTER 8: INFLUENCERS

1. Books you want to read:

2. Articles you want to read:

3. Podcasts/Webinars to listen and watch:

4. People to follow:

Thank you for joining me on this journey.

Patrice

Resources

Social media enables us to connect with researchers, leaders, and teachers around the globe. Because there is so much now available, it can be daunting to know where to look. Here are my top picks.

- Dr. Pooja Agarwal offers free guides, strategies, and research. In addition, she sends out a weekly newsletter to over 20,000 educators.

All of the resources on this page, and more, can be downloaded for free at Dr. Agarwal's site: www.retrievalpractice.org.

- Dr. Agarwal and I have a site www.powerfulteaching.org that also includes downloads of my strategies and other resources. If you are looking for research, you will find **10 recommended research articles on the science of learning**.

- Dr. Agarwal and I have a Powerful Teaching Book Study group at www.facebook.com/groups/powerfulteaching with several thousand global members. Join us!

The following resources offer both free and, for a fee, programs that can be used for individual growth and professional development. Although there are many resources available, these are the ones I consider my "go-to" for updated information:

- Evidence Based Education is a tremendous resource that offers case studies, webinars, reports, resources, and the Great Teaching Toolkit. https://evidencebased.education/

- InnerDrive is another tremendous resource. I particularly like, and have used, their graphic posters illuminating many science of learning topics. In addition, you will find webinars, blogs, studies, and *The Teaching & Learning Spotlight*, a quarterly magazine + webinar combination that explores the latest educational research. https://www.innerdrive.co.uk/

- Ross Morrison McGill is the creator of The Teacher Toolkit (https://www.teachertoolkit.co.uk/). His blog was named "one of the most influential blogs on education in the UK, winning the UK Blog Awards" and reaches over 17 million readers. In addition to his blogs, he features webinars along with many resources. I particularly like his Retrieval Practice Database for Teachers. https://www.teachertoolkit.co.uk/2024/02/25/retrieval-practice-database-for-teachers/

- The Center for Transformative Teaching & Learning (CTTL) has many resources and leads a Teacher Academy along with professional development for a cadre of teachers and schools. https://www.thecttl.org/

- Another source I highly recommend is the Federal Reserve Bank of St. Louis. At this site you will find economics classes and activities for all ages. One of the Instructional Designers is Andria Matzenbacher who, at the time of the research in my classroom, was my "next door" teacher who taught science and also became a part of the research studies. Her science of learning background can be found in many of the offerings at https://www.stlouisfed.org/education. For many years I was on the Educational Advisory Board for the Fed.

As an additional resource, I would also like to mention my book: *A Parent's Guide to Powerful Teaching.*[1] For K–12 students, parents play an important role and yet creating a learning partnership with them is often overlooked. In the *Parent's Guide,* I discuss the "Teaching Triangle," that important collaboration between student, parent, and teacher. Because the majority of parents have been through the educational system, they often encourage study strategies based upon those in which they are familiar. And yet, we as educators now know that many of those strategies are ineffective.

In conducting research for the *Parent's Guide,* I found the following. According to the United States National Center of Education Statistics[2] in the school year 2019–2020 there were:

- 50.8 million students in public schools
- 5.8 million students in private schools
- 3.7 million teachers

This means there are millions of students who do not have educators at home, and parents who aren't familiar with educational jargon or researched strategies that increase knowledge retention. If we want our students to be able to take advantage of all we know about learning, it is important to invite parents on this journey, to encourage the use of evidence-informed strategies at school and at home. The *Parent's Guide* offers the conversation that opens the collaboration.

Articles and Podcasts with Patrice Bain

If you are interested in more information, here are some of my articles and podcasts:

- International Society Technical Education (ISTE): How do I set my students up for success? (article/video) https://iste.org/blog/how-do-i-set-my-students-up-for-success

- Dr. Henry Roediger and Patrice Bain: Are you studying effectively? (St. Louis, Missouri NPR broadcast) https://www.stlpr.org/show/st-louis-on-the-air/2014-06-03/are-you-studying-effectively-what-wash-us-science-of-memory-tells-us-about-the-best-way-to-learn

- The value of applied research: Retrieval practice improves classroom learning and recommendations from a teacher, a principal, and a scientist. (article) https://psycnet.apa.org/record/2012-23428-008

- Cult of Pedagogy: Four research-based strategies all teachers should use. (podcast) https://www.cultofpedagogy.com/pod/episode-123/

- Annie Murphy Paul for *Scientific American*: Researchers find that frequent tests can boost learning. (article) https://www.scientificamerican.com/article/researchers-find-that-frequent-tests-can-boost-learning/

- Institute of Education Sciences: An example of the unquantifiable effect of research on practice. (article) https://ies.ed.gov/blogs/research/post/an-example-of-the-unquantifiable-effect-of-research-on-practice

- IgnitED Research Insight: Retrieval practice: Power tools for instruction. (article) https://practices.learningaccelerator .org/insights/retrieval-practice-power-tools-for-instruction-ignited-research-insight
- K–12 Dive: Trading in memorization for retrieval exercises can help quash students' internalized failure. (article) https://www .k12dive.com/news/trading-in-memorization-for-retrieval-exercises-can-help-quash-students-in/541462/
- EdSurge: The secret to student success? Teach them how to learn. (article) https://www.edsurge.com/news/2018-10-31-the-secret-to-student-success-teach-them-how-to-learn
- Teach Illinois: The importance of teaching metacognition (parts 1 and 2) with Patrice Bain. Host: Matt Weld. (podcast) https://www.teachillinois.com/podcast/archives/11-2018
- Naylor's Natter: Just talking to teachers. (UK podcast) https:// podcasters.spotify.com/pod/show/naylorsnatter/episodes/ Powerful-Teaching-with-Patrice-Bain-e4qs4p
- The Bedley Brothers: Powerful teaching with Patrice Bain. (podcast) https://www.podomatic.com/podcasts/bedleybros/ episodes/2019-10-12T02_00_00-07_00
- Teaching, Learning, Leading K–12: Powerful teaching with Patrice Bain. (podcast) https://teachinglearningleadingk12.pod bean.com/e/powerful-teaching-with-patrice-m-bain-265/
- Modern Classroom Project with Patrice Bain, Toni Rose Deanon, and Alison Stone (webinar)
- Teacher Toolkit (UK): Research informed retrieval practice with Patrice Bain. (podcast) https://www.teachertoolkit .co.uk/2019/11/17/podcast-62/?fbclid=IwAR3ks0KsllZiH2W 65FBMsGe6EY58tLjBXe8167W5Q9AAKPTFY6vF1fVVUyY

- Edutopia: Simple ways to integrate four evidence-based teaching strategies (article) https://www.edutopia.org/article/simple-ways-integrate-four-evidence-based-teaching-strategies?utm_content=buffer5f1bf&utm_medium=social&utm_source=linkedin.com&utm_campaign=buffer

- The Big R: Powerful language teaching. Host: Marek Tkaczyk, Poland. (webinar) https://www.youtube.com/watch?v=7Q-9QHC8i3Y

- InnerDrive: Cognitive Science origins: Being in the room where it happened. (UK article) https://www.innerdrive.co.uk/blog/cognitive-science-origins/

- Educational Neuroscience Hub: We as teachers are taught how to teach but it is really rare that we learn how our students learn, delving into the science of learning (parts 1 and 2). (podcast) https://educationalneurosciencehub.com/2023/07/09/we-as-teachers-are-taught-how-to-teach-but-it-is-really-rare-that-we-learn-how-our-students-learn-delving-into-the-science-of-learning-patrice-bain/

- Chalk and Talk: Powerful Teaching with Patrice Bain. Host: Anna Stokke. (Canada podcast) https://chalkandtalkpodcast.podbean.com/e/ep-13-powerful-teaching-with-patrice-bain/

- Vrain Waves: Hosts: Suzannah Evans and Shane Saeed (podcast) https://podcasts.apple.com/us/podcast/learning-is-a-party-make-sure-to-invite-your-students/id1365316994?i=1000631175495

- Fröjd's Toolbox: Host: Kennet Fröjd. (Sweden podcast, 1st minute in Swedish, then English) https://open.spotify.com/episode/10P5xgJD3VezDLVtyyYvC0

- Progressively Incorrect: The room where it happened. Host: Dr. Zach Groshell (podcast) https://podcasts.apple.com/us/podcast/s3e4-patrice-bain-on-the-room-where-it-happened/id1602317019?i=1000639284033

Podcasts discussing *A Parent's Guide to Powerful Teaching*:

- The Study Buddy: The learning parent: Applying principles of retrieval practice at home. Interview with Patrice Bain. Host: Nathan McGurl. (UK podcast) https://podcasts.apple.com/gb/podcast/learning-parent-applying-principles-retrieval-practice/id1501219828?i=1000502753092

- TLTalkRadio: Patrice Bain on *Powerful Teaching*. Host: Randy Ziegenfuss. (podcast) https://share.transistor.fm/s/c48d0d99

- Building the Bridge: Episode 7. Understanding how kids learn: An interview with Patrice Bain. Host: Wendy Oliver (podcast) https://podcasts.apple.com/us/podcast/episode-7-understanding-how-kids-learn-interview-patrice/id1536306968?i=1000501136438&hsCtaTracking=122b2105-7bc5-408c-8f74-5a9d09bd8a8d%7Cc855ee74-0928-4bf0-84f7-cf17ccc8b5e2

- Mind the Gap: Episode 14. *Powerful Teaching* for all with Patrice Bain. Hosts: Tom Sherrington and Emma Turner. (UK podcast) https://podcasts.apple.com/us/podcast/episode-14-powerful-teaching-for-all-with-patrice-bain/id1516532537?i=1000501693481

- Becoming Educated: Host: Darren Leslie (Scotland podcast) https://podcasts.apple.com/gb/podcast/the-teaching-triangle-with-patrice-bain/id1493757771?i=1000510121625

- The Principal Center: *A Parent's Guide to Powerful Teaching*. Host: Dr. Justin Baeder. (podcast) https://www.principalcenter.com/patrice-bain-a-parents-guide-to-powerful-teaching/

- 1 Huddle: Patrice Bain – Author of *Powerful Teaching: Unleash the Science of Learning*, Educator, Speaker. Host: Sam Caucci. (podcast) https://podcasts.apple.com/us/podcast/49-patrice-bain-author-of-powerful-teaching-unleash/id1511770027?i=1000529694582

- Dr. Kathy Weston's Get a Grip! Parenting Podcast: Dr. Weston talks with Patrice Bain. (UK podcast) https://podcasters.spotify .com/pod/show/dr-kathy-weston/episodes/Episode-99--- Dr-Weston-Talks-with-Patrice-Bain-A-Parents-Guide-to- Unleashing-Childrens-Learning-Potential-e1hkmlr
- Psychology in the Classroom: Powerful learning with Patrice Bain. Host: Lucinda Powell (UK podcast) https://changing statesofmind.com/podcast
- The Authority Podcast: *A Parent's Guide to Powerful Teaching* with Patrice Bain. Host: Ross Romano. (podcast) https:// authoritypodcast.net/episodes/a-parent-s-guide-to-powerful- teaching-with-patrice-bain-the-authority-podcast-69

The QR code is a link to my articles and podcasts.

NOTES

1. Bain, Patrice M., *A Parent's Guide to Powerful Teaching.* Woodbridge: John Catt Publishing, 2020.

2. National Center for Education Statistics. Back to school by the numbers: 2019–2020 school year. *NCES Blog*, August 13, 2019. Available at: https://nces.ed.gov/blogs/nces/post/back- to-school-by-the-numbers-2019-20-school-year [Accessed 26 April 2024].

About the Author

Patrice M. Bain, Ed.S., is a veteran K–12 and university educator, speaker, and author. As a finalist for Illinois Teacher of the Year and a Fulbright Scholar in Europe, she has been featured in national and international podcasts, webinars, presentations, and popular press, including *NOVA* and *Scientific American*. Bain provides professional development to teachers nationally and internationally. In addition to *Powerful Teaching*, she also co-authored an essential practice guide for educators: *Organizing Instruction and Study to Improve Student Learning*, in collaboration with the Institute of Education Sciences (IES). Bain's book *A Parent's Guide to Powerful Teaching* reinforces the "Teaching Triangle" of student, parent, and teacher collaboration. Patrice was one of two U.S. teachers on the working task group: *Neuromyths vs. Neurotruths*, sponsored by the IES and the National Commission of Educational Research (NCER). In addition, she was a contributor to the United Nations UNESCO ISEE (International Science and Evidence-based Education) Assessment, outlining the vision for world education by 2030.

About the Author

Index

Page references followed by *fig* indicated an illustrated figure.